Mule Deer
Western Challenge

Hunting Wisdom Library™

MINNETONKA, MINNESOTA

About the Author

For nearly two decades, Bob Robb's articles and photographs have appeared in most all the major hunting and fishing magazines. An avid outdoorsman and accomplished big game hunter with both firearms and bow, Bob has traveled the world on his big game hunting exploits. He has hunted mule deer and black-tails throughout their range, from Alaska and Canada down through the Rocky Mountain West, the Pacific coastal states and on into old Mexico. An editor for several national hunting magazines for 15 years, Bob is now a full-time freelance writer, member of the North American Hunting Club's Bowhunting Advisory Council, and an active participant in the fight against the anti-hunting movement. His previous books in this series include *Elk Essentials* and *Bowhunting Essentials*.

MULE DEER—WESTERN CHALLENGE

Printed in 2006.

Tom Carpenter
Creative Director

Jen Guinea
Heather Koshiol
Book Development Coordinators

Beowulf Ltd
Book Design and Production

David Rottinghaus
Illustrations

Dan Kennedy
Photo Editor

Phil Aarrestad
Commissioned Photography

North American Hunting Club
12301 Whitewater Drive
Minnetonka, Minnesota 55343
www.huntingclub.com

PHOTO CREDITS

Mike Francis: cover onlay; **Lee Kline:** title page, 19, 25, 33 (middle), 50, 81, 103 (top), 104 (bottom), 108, 110, 113, 123 (bottom),126, 131, 141, 146, 147 (bottom), 154 (bottom), 176; **Judd Cooney:** 8, 12 (top), 14, 33, 34 (top), 35 (bottom), 55 (bottom), 60, 76, 82, 86 (bottom), 88 (bottom), 102, 111, 128, 129 (top), 130, 132, 133, 178, 180 (bottom); **Tom Tietz:** 4, 6, 10, 11 (bottom), 13 (bottom), 16, 17, 18, 20, 24 (right), 25 (bottom), 30, 34 (bottom), 40, 41, 55 (top), 56 (top), 58, 61 (top), 66, 78, 79, 80, 84 (bottom), 85, 87 (top), 88 (top), 97 (bottom), 99, 101, 103 (bottom), 107, 112, 115, 127, 143, 145, 155, 156, 174, 179, 180 (top); **Donald Jones:** 11 (top), 28, 31, 44, 57, 63, 67, 68, 70, 71 (top), 72, 84 (top), 86 (top), 98 (top), 105 (top), 114, 124, 138, 139, 140, 153; **Animals Animals:** 12 (bottom), 119, 147 (top); **Eric Hansen:** 13 (top); **Bryce Towsley:** 27; **Bob Robb:** 29 (bottom), 47 (bottom), 48 (bottom), 54, 59, 62, 65, 89 (top), 90, 97 (top), 98 (bottom), 100, 116, 118, 120, 122, 123 (top), 144, 148, 159, 171 ; **Tom Carpenter/NAHC:** 32, 39 (bottom), 51, 83, 91, 96, 105 (bottom), 161, 162, 164, 166, 168, 170; **Dan Kennedy/NAHC:** 37 (top), 74, 157; **Tony Knight:** 43; **Ian McMurchy:** 46 (top); **Tom Fegely:** 49; **Mike Kraetsch:** 60; **Lee Lakosky:** 69; **Jack Barnes:** 87 (bottom), 104 (top), 177; **Tim Christie:** 106; **Jim Shockey:** 121; **Brad Herndon:** 152; **Jim Van Norman:** 21, 158, 182. Remaining photographs property of NAHC: 22, 26, 29 (top), 35 (top), 36, 37 (bottom), 38, 39, 42, 46 (bottom), 47 (top), 48 (top), 52, 56 (bottom), 61 (bottom), 64, 71 (bottom), 165.

Special Thanks To:
Boone and Crockett Club.® The Mule Deer Foundation.®

8 9 10 11 / 11 10 09 08 07 06
ISBN 1-58159-100-4
© 2000 North American Hunting Club

Table of Contents

Foreword

"Thirty inches, 30 inches, 30 inches" is the forlorn cry of the trophy mule deer hunter. The 30-inch standard for mule deer is probably the most recognizable and commonly accepted bench mark in all of big game hunting. And it's a shame. Mule deer have so much more to offer the hunter than just a big rack!

Now don't get me wrong; a mule deer buck that measures 30 inches from one side of its rack to the other is a tremendous animal, and it's a trophy worth anyone's time and effort to pursue. The problem is that the days of such bucks hiding behind every rock and cactus are long gone if they ever existed in the first place! A true, record-class mule deer may be the hardest of all trophy animals to find and hunt today.

Whether you travel to the West to hunt them or are fortunate enough to live there, expecting to take a "30-inch" mule deer means setting yourself up for major disappointment. But if you go afield with the expectation of enjoying the experience of hunting mule deer, then the 21st Century will hold a lot of hunting excitement and adventure for you.

Hunting mule deer is different than hunting any other big game animal. The beauty and diversity of the mule deer's West is a big part of that. You may be hunting real mountains with timber and snow, like you find in British Columbia, Idaho and Colorado. You may be hunting on rolling prairie and jagged badlands in ranching country like Montana and Wyoming and the Dakotas. You may hunt mule deer in truly agricultural lands like the wheat fields of Alberta and Washington State. You may even find yourself hunting mulies in the true desert in Sonora, Mexico, and parts of Utah, Arizona and Texas!

Frequently, mule deer hunting is hunting on the move. It's as real and as traditional Western-style glass-and-stalk hunting as you'll find anywhere. Even bowhunters can enjoy success by spotting a buck in his bed, then putting on a stocking-foot stalk. The mule deer will usually play the game in wide open country where you've got a chance to see him, but he's got a better chance to see you first.

If your measure of success in hunting is exclusively to kill a deer with a rack of some specific proportions, then please don't go mule deer hunting. In this day and age, you probably won't like it.

But if the size of the rack is secondary, and the real trophy you hope to take home is a memory of having experienced mule deer, mule deer country and mule deer hunting, then read on, enjoy and good luck in the hunt!

Best afield,

Bill Miller
Executive Director
North American Hunting Club

INTRODUCTION

*I*n the wide open spaces of the West, there is one big game animal that, to me, epitomizes everything that's great and good about the region. That animal is *Odocoileus hemionus hemionus*, the Rocky Mountain mule deer, and his family of subspecies including the black-tailed deer.

The West is a grand and beautiful land, at first glance appearing to be indestructible. The combination of vast, flat prairie and the continent's tallest, toughest mountain ranges gives the land a character of strength and grandeur. Its large rivers and crystal clear streams give it life. The timbered ridges and coastal forests are without peer. The West, so huge and awesome, appears incapable of being destroyed. And yet, as we know, even the West is fragile, bending under the hand of man until it begins to crack and break on many fronts.

The mule deer is a mirror of the modern West. A relative newcomer in geologic terms, mule deer are the product of whitetails and blacktails interbreeding in a land that time forgot. When, as a land, the West is strong and free, so too are the mule deer, whose numbers thrive and grow with the seasons. But when the land is soured, when habitat is destroyed and the very soul of the West is defiled, so too are mule deer. In this the two are as one: Mule deer and the land go hand in hand.

Modern game managers recognize this, and struggle to balance the needs of the growing Western people population with the needs of mule deer herds. These biologists know that if future generations are to see a sight that still, after more than 30 years of watching and hunting them, takes my breath away—a big-bodied mule deer buck, in the prime of life, with his tall, wide and heavy antlers outlined against a brilliant blue sky—they must carefully guard against habitat degradation and against overharvest by both human and natural predators. That task is not an easy one.

Mule deer hunting is more than mere sport or a way to put meat in the freezer. The more time you spend at it, the more you are able to recognize the subtleties of both the deer and the land that supports them. Soon you are no longer an intruder but a part of it all.

As a mule deer hunter, consistent success comes from knowing about these deer, their likes and dislikes, how they live, where they go during the different seasons. The more you hunt them, the more you realize there always is much more to learn.

Come along as we explore the world of the mule deer, and mule deer hunting. But first, a word of caution: Don't start unless you're prepared to be hooked. From the highest peaks to the lowest deserts, both the country and the mule deer have a way of seeping into your very soul.

—Bob Robb

Chapter 1

MULE DEER: WHAT ARE THEY?

*I*f you've never seen a mule deer before, or never hunted them, you may question your skills. I mean, everything you read or see about modern-day mulies makes them seem like some sort of super deer. And blacktails? Good grief, how can anyone ever find one of those little ghosts in that rain forest jungle? Obviously, you have never had a chance to learn first-hand what mule deer and blacktails are, how they act, where and how they live.

For folks like you, taking those first steps into the majestic world of the mule deer can be somewhat daunting. The country is big and intimidating. Before you even get started, you begin to have doubts about your ability. Where do I start looking? *How* do I look? Then, once you've seen some deer—does, probably, or yearling bucks—you might begin to wonder not just where, but *if,* there are any decent bucks around. It's easy to talk yourself out of success when faced with the unknown. That's one of the biggest reasons novice mule deer hunters rarely, if ever, take a mature buck on a self-guided hunt. Even you veteran mule deer hunters face some of these doubts.

Yet mule deer hunting remains one of the most popular Western hunting adventures. Together with resident hunters, many thousands of nonresidents have enjoyable, successful mule deer and blacktail hunts every fall. These are the serious handful of outdoorsmen and women who research their trips, scout when they can, and give themselves enough time in the field to tip the odds in their favor.

But it all begins with learning about mule deer and their smaller cousins, the blacktail—what they are, where and how they live, what they eat, how they react to different weather patterns and unwanted intrusions into their lives. This knowledge not only increases your chances of finding and then harvesting a good buck, but also increases the overall enjoyment of the hunt itself. Smart hunters—and mule deer hunters are no exception—find themselves becoming a part of the landscape, moving in harmony with the natural world into which they've ventured.

Are you as excited as I am? Then read on and learn more ...

HISTORY OF MULE DEER

Which came first, the chicken or the egg? In the case of mule deer, this famous rhetorical question can be paraphrased to something like, which deer came first, the mule deer or its close cousin, the blacktail? While the answers to such questions are based largely on speculation, today scientists believe the history of mule deer is a story of the meeting in the middle of two other deer species, the whitetail and the blacktail. To understand how this occurred, it is necessary to take a trip in the "Way Back Machine" and visualize what scientists tell us historically occurred, beginning some six million years ago.

Then, the New World's high Arctic was covered with forests, where it is believed that the first members of the family *Odocoileus*, our present-day deer species, lived. These early deer followed the creeping glacial edges southward. Fossil records indicate that the white-tailed and black-tailed deer appeared first. Whitetails spread slowly, appearing in North America for the first time an estimated one million years after their emergence. They first appeared on the West Coast, where they evolved into the black-tailed deer.

Due to the lack of high-quality food and an abundance of large predators, it was not until approximately 10,000 years ago that white-tailed and black-tailed deer became truly abundant, due to great changes in the available flora and prevalent fauna. Other mammals we find common in North America today—including the pronghorn, black

Scientists speculate that mule deer are really a cross between whitetails and black-tailed deer, both of which appeared first in the western reaches of the North American continent.

bear and coyote—became prevalent at the same time. Prior to this time, both whitetails and blacktails were limited in their ranges—the blacktail in the West and whitetail in the East—until changes in the continent's flora encouraged large-scale burning, which in turn created the large-scale sprouting of the new, young plants that deer thrive on.

Now, with an abundance of high-quality food and the absence of many of the large carnivores that helped keep their numbers down, deer began to spread their range. Before long, whitetails and black-tails met and interbred. It is this interbreeding that created the forerunners of modern mule deer. Scientists used the tools designed to determine heredity codes and, basing their theory on the DNA codes of the three different deer species, found this to be true. In fact, their research has shown that mule deer and whitetails have mitochondrial DNA—inherited through the female line, and thus, traceable as far back as you want to go—that is almost identical. The blacktail and whitetail, however, are far apart. Based on this evidence, their conclusion is that mule deer are the product of white-tail mothers and blacktail fathers.

Today mule deer dominate their home range, but share it on the fringes with both blacktails and whitetails. In fact, as we shall see later in this chapter, mule deer can and do inter-breed with both. The only North American deer species with which it has not shown it will interbreed is the tiny Coues' whitetail of the southwest, although the home ranges of the two also overlap to a small extent.

Modern mule deer may vary greatly in size, depending on where they live. However, Bergmann's Rule applies—the farther north you find the deer, the larger they are in body. Named mule deer for their oversized ears (which range from 4 to 7 inches in length), they stand between 3 and 3¹/₂ feet high at the shoulder, and measure between 3¹/₂ and 6 feet in length. Mature bucks vary in weight from 110 to 475 pounds, depending on where you find them, while does weigh between 75 and 200 pounds. What's realistic? A good, mature buck will weigh 200 to 225 pounds on the hoof, sometimes more; a doe, may be 140 or 150 pounds. Their tails are a giveaway; rope-like, mule deer tails are white above and tipped with black. True blacktails have a blackish tail with perhaps a bit of brown above. White-tailed deer's tails have no black.

Mule deer have evolved into several different subspecies. To learn more about them, turn the page and read on.

Mule deer made their appearance relatively recently on the evolutionary calendar.

MULE DEER SUBSPECIES

Over the years there's been quite a debate regarding exactly how many mule deer subspecies there are, and where these subspecies live. At one time there were thought to be 11 distinct subspecies. Today taxonomists recognize 8. Although generally no longer recognized, two subspecies—the burro and Inyo mule deer—still have their proponents.

Rocky Mountain mule deer.

1 The **Rocky Mountain mule deer** (*Odocoileus hemionus hemionus*) is the most common subspecies, has the largest home range and is the most populous. It ranges roughly from the southern edge of the Northwest Territories down through British Columbia, Alberta, Saskatchewan and western Manitoba through the western Dakotas, Montana, Idaho and eastern Washington, then south through western Oregon and northwestern California, Nevada, Utah, Wyoming, Colorado and the northern and central portions of Arizona and New Mexico. Its range also spreads into portions of western Nebraska, Oklahoma and Texas. It is also the largest bodied of the mule deer subspecies.

2 The **California mule deer** (*O. h. californicus*) is found only in California, ranging roughly from the Sierra Nevada Mountains west to the Pacific Ocean. Along the northern and western borders of its range, it interbreeds with the Columbia blacktail.

California mule deer have smaller bodies and antlers than the Rocky Mountain muley, with antlers that often achieve only a forked-horn shape.

3 The **Southern mule deer** (*O. h. fuliginatus*) is found along the southern California coast, from roughly Los Angeles County south into Baja California. It is about the same size as the California mule deer, but usually much darker.

4 The **Inyo mule deer** (*O. h. inyoensis*) is a disputed subspecies, located in and around Inyo County, California, on the eastern slope of the Sierra Nevada Mountains. Many taxonomists simply call this deer a version of the California mule deer.

5 The **burro deer** (*O. h. eremicus*) is thought by many to be a form of the desert mule deer. Its range is the extreme southeastern desert of California and southwestern desert of Arizona, ranging down into northern Sonora, Mexico, and the extreme northeastern corner of the Baja Peninsula. It is a small deer, and lighter in color than other subspecies.

Desert mule deer.

6   The **desert mule deer** (*O. h. crooki*) has the second largest distribution of all the mule deer subspecies. It ranges from the deserts of southeastern Arizona, southern New Mexico and western Texas down hundreds of miles into Sonora, Mexico. It is a large-boned and long-legged deer, but thin through the withers. It lives in some of the harshest habitat imaginable, with little water and scant forage.

7   The **Columbia blacktail** (*O. h. columbianus*) is found in a narrow coastal band stretching from north-central California up through Oregon, Washington and British Columbia, as well as on Canada's Vancouver Island. It lives in a variety of habitat in this area, ranging from dry chaparral, to oak/grassland, to the densest, thickest and wettest coastal rain forests. These deer have a more reddish coat than other mule deer subspecies, shorter ears and an all-black tail.

8   The **Sitka blacktail** (*O. h. sitkensis*) lives only on British Columbia's Queen Charlotte Islands and the coastal mainland and islands of Alaska, including Kodiak, the large ABC chain—Admiralty, Baranof and Chichagof islands—and the massive Prince of Wales

Columbia blacktail buck.

Island as well as smaller adjacent islands. Sitka deer have short, blocky bodies, short, thick antlers and a cinnamon-brown coat.

Two other small subspecies of mule deer are sometimes referred to as well. These are the **Tiburon Island** and **Cedros Island mule deer**, although many people believe they are members of the desert and southern subspecies, respectively.

In my life I've been fortunate to observe and hunt all the different mule deer subspecies. Growing up in southern California, I hunted the California, Southern, burro and Inyo subspecies regularly, finally traveling far enough north to hunt the Columbia blacktail. During college I began making trips to northeastern California and many other western states to pursue the Rocky Mountain mule deer. Finally I hit the extremes, hunting both the desert mule deer and Sitka blacktail. Over the past 30 years I've hunted at least one mule deer subspecies each year—usually it's been two or more. Those experiences have given me a deep appreciation for each, as well as the challenges they present.

Sitka blacktail buck.

Mule Deer: What Are They?

Mule Deer Senses & Personality

Jim Van Norman is an outfitter, guide, rancher and outdoor writer from Edgerton, Wyoming. You'll find his insights and advice—on mulies and hunting them— sprinkled throughout this book.

A mule deer's senses are as acute as any deer species. A buck's eyes, ears and nose are among the incredible tools he uses to evade predators—human or otherwise. But they're not the only tools, as you'll see.

Mule Deer Radar—A mule deer's eyes are excellent, even at great distance. In fact, I put them in the same category as a pronghorn's. I can't tell you how many times I've been glassing only to find a mule deer about a mile away, bedded and looking right back at me. Mule deer eyes also are very sensitive to movement, no matter how small or minute, at distances you wouldn't

believe. This is why it is so important to stay out of sight of the country you are glassing, as you hunt. And a mule deer's peripheral vision is extreme. He is able to detect the slightest movement around a 360-degree circle, especially at close range, with very little effort. A modern radar screen has very little advantage over the eyes of a mule deer.

Mule Deer Sonar—The mule deer's prominent ears are at the top of the list when it comes to major defenses. Mule deer swivel their ears around almost continuously, listening in different directions for anything disturbing. I've even

Mule deer vision and hearing are incredibly acute. Be seen or heard and you probably won't get a second chance.

noticed, after making an inadvertent noise while stalking up on mule deer, that they will swivel their ears almost in reverse to listen directly behind themselves. Some mule deer (especially big bucks) trust their ears enough that, having heard a disturbing noise, they will get up and quietly leave the area long before trouble has a chance to show up—even when they haven't seen or smelled anything.

Mule Deer "Nose-ar"—If I had to pick one sense that a mule deer depends on continuously, it would be his nose. Mulies are constantly evaluating the air. Big bucks will sometimes spend many daylight hours lying down in a washout or gully where there's no way to see or hear anything coming before it gets extremely close. But they always seem to position themselves where the wind is in their favor. Although a mule deer may see you at a great distance and choose to stay bedded, or may hear you and wait to see what is coming, he will *never* wait around once he has winded you. Evaluating the wind properly when hunting mule deer is a must.

Which sense does a mule deer prefer? Here's a common scenario: A buck prefers to position himself with a panoramic view in front, to be able to see an intruder coming. Yet he hides well, so that he can hear warnings of danger from any compass direction. And when bedded, he likes the wind at his back so he can smell what he can't see or hear.

Mule Deer Personality—A "well-seasoned" mule deer uses his senses as well as any whitetail, anywhere. It's true! By well-seasoned, I mean that the ability a mule deer develops to be elusive is directly proportionate to his experience escaping danger. The more an individual deer escapes, the better he or she gets at the skill. This general evasiveness, along with the deer's eyes, ears and nose, creates a personality made for survival. The older a mule deer is, the tougher he is to kill.

Personality transfers from mother to young and

Mule deer are always using—and trusting—their noses.

from old buck to young buck. It's sort of like with people. If the parents and friends are "whacko," so are the kids. If grandpa or grandma are nuts and are helping raise the kids, the siblings are "twisted" too. Similarly, I have known many paranoid bucks. Generally referred to as "loners" or "ridge runners" or most commonly "the [expletive] that got away again," these types of bucks generally live alone, are nocturnal and seldom stop—once spooked—for any reason! The problem is, *everything* spooks them—near or far.

There is nothing that makes bigger, older mule deer bucks harder to get close to than fine, highly developed senses, plenty of experience and a paranoid personality. Paying attention to all details, respecting the mule deer's sharpened senses and knowing his quirky, paranoid makeup will net you more big bucks than the average hunter, guaranteed.

—Jim Van Norman

ALL ABOUT ANTLERS

Antlers have fascinated human hunters since we made our homes in caves. Dr. Richard Goss, an authority on antler regeneration, has called them "a biological extravagance ... so highly improbable that if they had not evolved in the first place, they would never have been conceived of even in the wildest fantasies of the most imaginative biologist."

Only members of the deer family grow antlers, and except for caribou and reindeer, only males grow them. Pedicles—short, stubby extensions of the frontal bone—are developed on the top of the skull before birth. From here antlers grow annually, beginning the cycle each spring until they are shed in winter. Antlers are made from calcium, phosphorous and other minerals, and exhibit the fastest-known bone growth. While growing they are covered in "velvet," a specialized skin containing numerous blood vessels.

In this condition they are very soft and tender. Antler growth is linked to the increasing amounts of daylight that occur as spring stretches into summer.

Mule deer have what biologists call "bifurcated" antlers, defined by Webster's as "divided into two branches or parts." This refers to the fact that normal (typical) mule deer antlers branch from each tine that emerges, thus creating the typical double-forked, or 4-points-per-side mule deer rack. Mule deer also generally have eye guards, though these are not nearly as prominent as those found on whitetails. However, mule deer can and do develop "non-typical" antler configurations, with many points sprouting off in different directions. And,

Typical mule deer have what scientists call "bifurcated" antlers, meaning that bucks have antlers that branch, or fork, from each tine that emerges. Some old monarchs have lots of "trash" points (which hunters love), making them non-typicals.

in some areas, a large number of mature mule deer and blacktail bucks are seen with antlers more typical of whitetails, that is, antlers with a single main beam and two long points sprouting off it. This antler configuration is not uncommon a for Columbia blacktails in portions of their range, and Sitka blacktails throughout their range, for example.

Antler size is determined by three things: diet, genetics and age. Deer must have a diet rich in both protein and the minerals needed to grow big antlers.

The deer must also come from a genetic stock that can produce big antlers. And a buck must grow old enough to reach his full potential to achieve oversized antlers. However, keep in mind that big antlers do not necessarily mean an old buck, and vice versa.

A buck will grow his largest antlers when he's in the prime of his life, somewhere between ages five and eight, depending on several factors. Mule deer have been known to live as long as 15 years in captivity, but a 10-year-old in the wild is an old man indeed. Once

Mule Deer: What Are They?

bucks reach their physical peak and continue to age, their antlers often begin to deteriorate, retaining their mass but growing stunted points. They may add or even lose points. Two of the largest bucks I've ever seen were old-timers, one with thick, wide antlers with 6 stunted points per side, the other a giant non-typical I shot in Sonora that had a 34½-inch spread and 16 scorable points branching off what appeared to be a whitetail main beam. You never know.

While you often hear hunters talk about what a deer "scored" according to the record book, just because a buck's antlers do not score well does not mean he isn't a monster. The best bucks I've ever seen have antlers that just don't quite fit the "book's" definition of a high-scoring rack, yet they were tall, wide and massive, often with several small "trash" points that actually hurt the book score. In truth, these are the kinds of muley antlers I like the most. I get chills every time I see one.

But in the end, any mule deer you decide to take is a trophy. Because he or she is a fascinating animal indeed, and the country you hunted in was certainly memorable.

To score well by record book definitions, a muley needs heavy symmetrical antlers with long tines and deep forks. Overall antler size is determined by three things: age, genetics and diet.

The Records

Bill Barcus and his Pope & Young world record mule deer.

The Boone and Crockett Club's 10th edition record book shows that the number one typical mule deer was taken by Doug Burris Jr., in 1972 in Dolores County, Colorado. It has an inside spread of 30$^7/_8$ inches, a 5x6 rack, and scores 226$^4/_8$ points. The number one non-typical mule deer was taken by Ed Broder near Chip Lake, Alberta, in 1926. This buck had an inside spread of only 22$^1/_8$ inches, but an incredible 22x21 rack that scores 355$^2/_8$ points. The minimum typical B&C score is 195 points, the non-typical minimum 240 points.

The top B&C Columbia blacktail scores 182$^2/_8$ points, has an inside spread of 20$^2/_8$ inches, and a 5x5 rack. It was taken by Lester Miller in Lewis County, Washington, in 1953. The top B&C Sitka blacktail scores 128 points, sports a 5x5 rack and an inside spread of 19$^4/_8$ inches. It was taken by an unknown hunter on Kodiak Island, Alaska, in 1985, and is now owned by Craig Allen. The minimum B&C Columbia blacktail score is 135 points, while the minimum Sitka blacktail score is 108 points.

According to the 1993 edition of the Pope and Young Club record book, the world record typical mule deer with bow and arrow was taken by Bill Barcus in 1979 in the White River National Forest, Colorado. The buck had an inside spread of 30$^2/_8$ inches, 7 points per side, and scores 203$^1/_8$ points. The world record non-typical buck was taken in 1987 from Morgan County, Colorado, by Kenneth Plank. It has an inside spread of 27 inches, 35 scorable points, and scores 274$^7/_8$. The minimum P&Y typical score is 145 points, and 160 points for non-typical antlers.

The archery world record typical Columbia blacktail was taken in Marion County, Oregon, by B.G. Shurtleff in 1969. It has 7 points per side, an inside spread of 20$^4/_8$ inches, and scores 172$^2/_8$ points. The top non-typical has 18 scorable points, an inside spread of 19$^1/_8$ inches, and scores 194$^4/_8$ points. It was taken by James Decker in 1988 in Jackson County, Oregon. (This buck scored almost 50 points more than the number two buck, which scored 146$^0/_8$ points and was taken in 1984 in San Mateo County, California.) The minimum score for typical antlers is 90 points, and 110 points for non-typical antlers.

The top Pope and Young Sitka buck scores 116$^3/_8$ points, has a 5x5 rack and inside spread of 13$^1/_8$ inches, and was taken by Charles Hakari on Prince of Wales Island, Alaska, in 1987. The minimum P&Y score is 65 points.

HYBRID DEER

Along the fringes of its home range, mule deer can, and do, interbreed with both other mule deer subspecies and with whitetails. Wherever mule deer meet whitetails, muley popu- lations show a tendency to shrink. According to noted mule deer expert Dr. Valerius Geist, this is not due to the deer "competing" for food or material things like escape cover and terrain. In fact, it is not

all that unusual in some areas to see mule deer and whitetails feeding within sight of each other in river-bottom areas or on the winter range. Instead, shrinking muley populations are due to what Geist has called "one-way hybridization."

In a nutshell: More mature whitetail bucks are available for breeding in a given area than mature mule deer bucks. This is because mature muley bucks are more often killed by human hunters than are the more nocturnal, secretive mature whitetail bucks.

Mature whitetail bucks are more aggressive breeders than their mule deer counterparts. A whitetail buck will chase down and mate with estrus muley does.

These larger whitetail bucks displace the remaining younger mule deer bucks, permitting the whitetail bucks to breed mule deer does. Geist believes that mule deer bucks rarely, if ever, breed with whitetail does, because when approached by any buck during breeding season, whitetail does are prone to run (mule deer does normally do not run), and it is extremely difficult for muley bucks to catch the faster whitetail does.

Hybrid deer are often quickly recognizable. I remember the first one I ever saw, in eastern Montana's Missouri Breaks region in the mid-1980s. We saw several does that had the blocky body and distinctive bounding gait of a mule deer—but they sported whitetail tails and ears. We also saw two young bucks that had mule deer bodies and ran like mulies, but had faces that appeared more like whitetails, including short ears and a shorter snout, along with a distinctive whitetail

rack and tail. They're strange looking critters indeed.

In addition to mule deer/whitetail hybrids, different subspecies of mule deer will interbreed, creating a cross. This is quite common where mule deer and blacktail herds come together. Along the dividing line established by the various record books to delineate mule deer and Columbia blacktail ranges, I've seen some huge bucks with all the outward appearances of blacktails, but with bodies and antlers simply too large not to have some Rocky Mountain mule deer influence. At the southern end of the blacktail range in central California, blacktails and California mule deer freely interbreed. The late Don Pine, a biologist for the California Department of Fish & Game, used to take me to places where we could see deer that exhibited the distinct physical characteristics of blacktails; then in the next canyon, he'd show me deer that displayed the distinct characteristics of California mule deer. These deer freely intermingle and crossbreed at will.

When it comes time to breed, deer obviously pay no attention to the arbitrary record-book lines drawn by man.

Mostly out on the plains and prairies, in places like Colorado and Montana and Wyoming, you might find yourself an interesting "combo" buck like this one.

Chapter 2

CHOOSE YOUR WEAPON

Serious mule deer hunters are also serious shooters. I have yet to meet a group of hunters who are more concerned with the nuances of their rifles, bows, muzzleloaders and handguns than dedicated mule deer addicts.

Over the years, muley hunters learn that opportunities at really good bucks don't come often. In fact, there can be many seasons in between chances at really good bucks, if those chances come at all. And when those opportunities do arise, they are not always under the best of circumstances. For one thing, the weather can be less than cooperative. There can be rain, sleet or snow falling thick enough to cause poor visibility. A stiff crosswind that bounces your sight picture like a rubber ducky in rough water—and drives your bullet or arrow unpredictably off target—isn't unheard of. Steep downhill and uphill angles are common.

Then there are the distances at which hunters commonly take mule deer. If you're an east-of-the-Mississippi River whitetail hunter, you probably think that anything over 150 yards is "way out there." Bowhunters who ply their trade from treestands rarely shoot past 30 yards (and more commonly half that distance). In mule deer country it's a whole 'nother game. Bow shots under 30 yards are cherished. And while most mulies taken with a rifle are shot at 200 yards or less, there are times when a shot of twice that distance is the only chance you get—whether or not to take it is another subject.

To make these shots when the opportunity arises requires a combination of skill developed through consistent practice, familiarity with one's weapon, and a gun-and-load or bow-and-arrow combination that's been finely tuned to work together in close harmony.

Mule deer hunters are serious about every facet of the game. But, above all else, they know that when all their planning and hard work finally come together, and their fantasy buck presents that one opportunity they've been dreaming of day and night for so long, they must be able to make the shot.

As James Russell Lowell wrote in his classic work *The Vision of Sir Launfal* in 1848, "And what is so rare as a day in June? Then, if ever, come perfect days." For modern mule deer hunters, finding that dream buck is as rare as those perfect days.

When it all comes together, you want to make the shot count. Here's what you need—and need to do—to get the job done ...

GUNS & LOADS

When it comes to hunting mule deer, most people think in terms of extreme long-range shooting across a vast canyon or a flat sagebrush plain. In truth, most mulies are taken at close to moderate distances of a couple hundred yards or less. However, there is always the chance that the buck of your dreams will appear in the distance, and the only opportunity you'll have is a longer shot. Shots can also be at steep uphill or downhill angles that can be tricky.

For these reasons mule deer hunters are as finicky about their rifles as any group of big game hunters anywhere. Experienced and ethical deer hunters also believe reverently that making that first shot count, regardless of distance or conditions, is the most important aspect in hunting. To that end, carrying afield an accurate rifle that you have learned to shoot well under field conditions is crucial to both your enjoyment and your success as a mule deer hunter.

A bolt action rifle offers the ruggedness and accuracy you need in mule deer country.

RIFLE ACTIONS

While there are several different rifle action types—including pump, autoloading, and lever actions—the two most accurate, and therefore the most appropriate for most all mule deer hunting—are the bolt-action and falling-block single-shot. Generally speaking, these rifles come in the widest selection of cartridge chamberings, allowing you to select exactly the cartridge you wish. They usually have the best triggers, an often

No matter what rifle you're carrying, take the time to find and use a rest for every shot.

overlooked but critically important aspect of an accurate deer rifle. They come in the widest selection of barrel lengths, stock materials and overall weight. All are drilled and tapped to accept scope mounts.

There are some fine single-shot rifles out there these days. Ruger, Browning, Thompson/Center and H&R make the most popular, but there are others. Don't pooh-pooh single-shots because they have no fast follow-up shot. In mule deer hunting, the first shot is everything. If you miss it, it simply means you weren't close enough or didn't take enough time to get ready. If the shot is a quick one before the deer disappears over the crest of the mountain or into the brush, a machine gun wouldn't have helped.

Bolt actions are by far the most popular for mule deer hunters. Today so many good ones are out there that it's simply a matter of picking one that fits your needs. Many superb, accurate rifles are available over the counter—rifles that have more than enough accuracy and will last you a lifetime. Remington, Winchester, Browning, Ruger, Weatherby, Sako, Savage, Marlin and Dakota are some of the more recognizable names. All are backed by excellent warranties, have easily obtainable parts, and you can get them repaired if necessary at most neighborhood gun shops. All my mule deer rifles are bolt actions, save one, a single-shot.

Don't scrimp on your scope. Buy a notch above what you can afford. You'll add minutes to your hunting time and will make more shots count.

STOCKS, SLINGS & BARRELS

Stocks are much better today than they were 20 years ago. Today's are designed to provide maximum comfort when shooting a scoped rifle. They fit the

Synthetic stocks (top), which are better choices in wet, snowy, frigid weather, are fast replacing traditional wooden stocks on mule deer rifles.

Today most factory rifles come with accurate barrels assembled into actions and bedded into stocks that can produce 3-shot groups at 100 yards of 1½ inches or so with factory ammunition. This is great performance! I can remember many years ago when we worked like the dickens with handloads to get out rifles to shoot that well! If you want even better accuracy, an after-market barrel like those from Shilen, Hart, McMillan and Douglas is the way to go.

In terms of barrel length, the longer the barrel the better, within reason, simply because the longer barrel allows the entire powder charge to be consumed before exiting; this adds velocity to the bullet. Most mule deer hunters use rifles with barrels measuring between 22 and 24 inches, though some short-action mountain-type rifles have 20-inch barrels and some magnum-caliber rifles have 26-inch barrels. The really short barrels make no sense if used on magnum cartridges like the 7mm Rem. Mag., for example, because a lot of the powder will not be burned before the

average-sized man well, provide a sure grip, and secure the action, while keeping the barrel from contacting the stock, which can cause inaccurate bullet flight. Most come with a quality recoil pad, but you can add inexpensive after-market pads that reduce felt recoil even more.

Today you can choose from either traditional wooden stocks or stocks made from synthetic materials like Fiberglass, Kevlar and others. While I still love the way a fine wooden stock looks and feels, all my serious deer rifles sport synthetic stocks. Synthetic stocks are inert; that is, they don't change shape in wet, cold or extremely hot weather the way wood can, which can adversely affect accuracy. Although some old-style synthetic stocks are as heavy as wood, most are lighter, while soaking up more of the felt recoil at the same time. I don't care if I scratch them up during seasons of hard hunting. In my mind, they're the only way to go.

Mule deer hunters need a rifle sling. And while traditional leather slings look great and do the job, a neoprene sling is lighter and much more comfortable to carry. That's because the neoprene material actually "gives" with each step, soaking up some of the shock. Also, flexible neoprene slings are much easier to wrap tightly into when shooting with a tight sling, something all serious mule deer hunters should know how to do. One of Butler Creek's superb neoprene slings can be found on all my mule deer rifles.

The most important part of a rifle is its barrel.

Butler Creek's superb neoprene rifle slings are excellent choices for mule deer hunting. Unlike leather and canvas slings, they help soak up the load with each step you take.

Sighting In for Mule Deer Hunting

Sight in carefully and completely using solid rifle rests both fore and aft, at a rifle range. Accuracy equals confidence, which breeds success.

Because most mule deer cartridges sport a relatively flat trajectory, they should be sighted in to hit between 2½ and 3 inches high at 100 yards. That will allow you to aim right on the deer's chest from point blank range to around 250 to 325 yards and hit the vitals, depending on the cartridge you're using. Finding the exact trajectory of your cartridge is easy. Many boxes of factory ammunition have trajectory tables printed right on them. There are also books available that more specifically show this. The best way, though, is to use one of the many computer ballistics programs available. RCBS, Barnes and Sierra produce excellent programs of this type.

Sight in your rifle at the range using a sturdy bench rest with both front and back rifle rests. First check to make sure that all screws, including those on your scope mounts, are tight. After putting on ear and eye protection, sit down, get comfortable with both feet flat on the ground. Rest the rifle's forend (not the barrel!) on the front rest; let the back of the stock lie on the rear rest. Adjust these rest positions until the crosshairs are right on the bull's eye. Take your time, control your breathing, and squeeze off a shot. Wait 30 to 60 seconds, then shoot again. Wait, then shoot a third time. Now adjust the scope as indicated by the target, and repeat. After three groups I clean my barrel before continuing.

After sighting in the rifle, I thoroughly clean the barrel. I also save my target and store it with my rifle, so that when it's time to head afield I can glance at it and quickly know exactly where my rifle is shooting. All this may seem like unnecessary nit-picking, but when the deer of your dreams suddenly appears, you won't have to worry about where your rifle is shooting. You'll simply place the crosshairs on his chest, squeeze the trigger and then punch your tag.

bullet leaves the barrel. You'll lose too much velocity and add a lot of unnecessary recoil.

RIFLE SCOPES

Equally as important as the rifle you choose for hunting mule deer is the scope you select. As is the case with factory rifles, today's rifle scopes are the finest ever offered, at prices anyone can afford.

Buy the best scope you can afford. Period. Mule deer hunting often takes place in lousy weather, and the last thing you need is a scope that fogs up in the rain or loses its optical quality after a few dings. Bausch & Lomb, Zeiss, Leica and Swarovski make superb scopes. Nikon, Simmons and Weaver make fine scopes too, for less money.

Variable power scopes received a bad rap in their infancy, but today I don't own anything else. Scopes in the 2.5-8X, 2.5-10X, 3-9X, 3-12X and 4-14X are common sights on modern mule deer rifles. Make sure your scope gathers enough available light to permit shooting at dawn and dusk. I find that an objective

lens size of 40mm or so provides a good compromise between light-gathering ability, size and weight.

Also, make sure to mount your scope in bulletproof scope mounts. After having the large rear scope-holding screw vibrate loose on a Redfield-type scope mount years ago, today I use nothing except mounts that securely lock the rings in place with set screws both fore and aft. While there are others, Conetrol makes the best mounts of this type I've ever used.

WHICH CARTRIDGE IS BEST?

Forget everything you've read about whiz-bang cartridges that shoot flat as a pancake until they fall off the curve of the earth. For most mule deer hunting, a medium velocity cartridge is all you really need. In this, it is hard to argue with the .30-06 or .270.

There are others, of course. In general, the best deer hunting cartridges have a bore size between .243 and .308. The list includes the .243 Win., 6mm Rem., .240 Wthby Mag., .257 Roberts, .25-06 Rem., .257 Wthby Mag., .264 Win. Mag., .284 Win., .280 Rem., 7mm-08

Buy the very best quality rifle scope you can for a mule deer rifle. Your scope will need to perform flawlessly in all sorts of bad weather, including rain, snow and dusty conditions. Medium-power variable models, like 2X-7X, are the most popular today.

For most mule deer hunting, medium velocity cartridges with a bore size between .243 and .308 are all you really need. The .270, .30-06 and .308 are the three most popular.

difficult to kill cleanly. However, there are times when shot angles are poor, and that can require a stoutly constructed bullet that will penetrate deeply, retain nearly all of its original weight, and transfer the bulk of its kinetic energy to the animal before exiting (should it do so). The bullet should also handle impact with medium-sized bones. And because mule deer can be shot at distances ranging from 40 yards to 400 yards or more, the bullet must perform well over this entire spectrum.

That's asking a lot! Fortunately, today's users of factory ammunition can find the world's best bullets already loaded for them in ammunition that is as accurate—or nearly so—as the handloads we created 20 years ago. These include the Nosler Partition and Partition Gold, Winchester Fail Safe, Barnes X-Bullet, Trophy Bonded Bear Claw, Swift A-Frame and Speer Grand Slam. Some old favorites work very well on mule deer too. These include the Remington Core-Lokt, Winchester Power Point and Silvertip, Sierra Boattail and Spitzer, and Hornady Interlock. Because modern-day hunters demand the finest in performance, sales of "premium" brands of factory ammunition have sky-rocketed in recent years. And rightly so. This gives the user the best bullets in the world loaded

Rem., 7x57 Mauser, 7mm Rem. Mag., 7mm Wthby Mag., .308 Win., .300 H&H Mag., .300 Win. Mag. and .300 Wthby Mag. Any of these will get the job done. I've shot more mule deer with the .270 Win., .280 Rem. and .30-06 than any others, though today my deer rifle is the custom-built .300 Win. Mag. mentioned below.

More important than caliber is the bullet. Mule deer are not overly large animals, nor are they all that

Custom Rifles

*T*he market for custom rifles has never been stronger. Many modern hunters feel that an investment of between $2,400 and $5,000 for a super-accurate, lightweight rifle is money well spent.

While factory rifles will produce all the performance most mule deer hunting calls for, I splurged a few years ago and had a custom rifle built for mountain hunting. At the time I wondered why I was wasting so much money. Now, after several seasons of very tough field use in hunting a variety of mountain game, my only regret is that I didn't do it sooner. This rifle, chambered for the .300 Win. Mag., produces sub-2-inch, 5-shot groups at 250 yards. It is this kind of accuracy that instills confidence that when I squeeze the trigger, it's time to reach for my skinning knife. Every time.

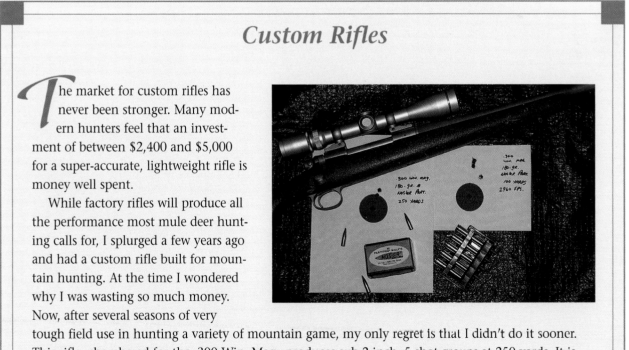

at the factory, with the world's best components to tolerances previously unknown. Mule deer hunters have never had it so good.

HOW ACCURATE IS ACCURATE ENOUGH?

These days, it is not too difficult to get one of today's factory bolt-action or single-shot rifles to shoot a particular brand of factory ammunition into three-shot clusters measuring 1¹/₂ inches at 100 yards. For most mule deer hunting, 1¹/₂-inch accuracy is good enough.

Producing better accuracy takes time and work. You might need to bed your barrel, work over the trigger, install a custom barrel, and so on. It takes time and a fair chunk of change. You might have to handload, custom-tailoring your ammunition to your rifle.

But I've found that I can make almost all factory rifles shoot near 1-inch groups with minor tinkering. The process usually involves properly breaking in the barrel (cleaning it before shooting it, cleaning it after each shot for the first 20 shots, and cleaning it after every two shots for the next 20, all the while cooling it down between shots), then experimenting with several different brands of factory ammunition and different bullet weights to see what it likes best. After all's said and done, there are generally one or two factory loads the rifle seems to prefer above all others, and these usually group somewhere between 1 and 1¹/₂ inches.

One often-overlooked factor in the accuracy equation is barrel maintenance. It is very, very important to keep the barrel clean, removing all fouling from the barrel to prevent a buildup that will, over time, erode accuracy. On the range, I clean my barrel every 15 to 20 shots, then I really scour it before putting it away after each session. If you've never followed this procedure, you'll be amazed at how it will improve your rifle's accuracy. There is a right way and a wrong way to clean your barrel too. Ask your local gunsmith how to go about it.

With proper bullet placement, mule deer are not overly large nor terribly difficult animals to kill cleanly with a modern centerfire rifle. However, smart buck hunters use the best bullets loaded in top-of-the-line factory ammunition—or their own handloads—to prevent poor performance at the moment of truth.

Wind Drift

Wind drift can affect bullet flight in mule deer country, especially at long ranges. To eliminate potential problems, use spitzer-type bullets, take a solid rest and close the range as much as possible before shooting.

One year I spent a lot of time around Olympic rifle shooters. These people make their living by "doping the wind" and then adjusting their point of aim so that the wind will push their slow .22 ammunition into the bull's eye. They know that a crosswind definitely will affect their bullet's flight path.

Unless you spend an inordinate amount of time shooting in windy country with the same rifle and ammunition combination, learning to dope the wind like these folks is impossible. As a mule deer hunter, you need to know two things: a stiff crosswind can throw your shot off target; and in mule deer country, it seems like the wind always blows.

You can make adjustments fairly easily, though. First, always use spitzer or spitzer/boattail-type bullets; these are the most aerodynamically designed and least prone to

the effects of the wind. Second, always take a solid rest before shooting. Taking a rest, especially one low to the ground, will keep the wind from moving the rifle as you aim and shoot, which can throw the shot off. Third, study wind drift tables for your load. These can be found on many ammunition boxes, as well as some computer ballistics programs. Fourth, when the wind is really blowing, get as close to the deer as possible before shooting. The closer you are, the less wind can affect bullet flight. Fifth, and perhaps most important: If you're not sure about the shot, don't take it.

On windy days, you often can stalk very close, because a steady wind will cover the sound of your approach and take your scent the other way. Use this to your advantage, get right in his lap, take a solid rest, squeeze the trigger and get out the skinning knife.

Bows & Arrows

Steve Seitz of Georgia is typical of the many eastern bowhunters I've run into in the mountains of the West. A man who had some hunting experience under his belt, Steve had taken whitetails and wild boars from treestands in the South, but had never before bowhunted big game from the ground.

His shooting skills and his bowhunting equipment were eastern-oriented. Steve had never made a shot on game farther than 30 yards, which he considered reaching out a bit. After the second day of hunting and several encounters with muley bucks, Steve realized that he was going to have to learn to shoot past the 30-yard mark if he was going to take one of the many nice bucks running around this New Mexico ranch. And so he and I spent two hours during a midday break resighting in his bow, then practicing shooting at 40 and 50 yards at a life-sized mule deer 3-D target. It wasn't long before he was placing his shafts in the kill zone every shot, and his confidence soared.

On the next to last day of the hunt, Steve and his guide found a dandy 4x4 buck feeding along the edge of an open alfalfa field. After a careful stalk, Steve's guide used his rangefinder and dialed in the distance. Steve made a letter-perfect 43-yard shot, and soon celebrated a trophy that even veteran mule deer bowhunters would be proud to tag.

Practicing until you can make a 40-yard shot will definitely up your odds on a mule deer bow hunt.

STRETCH YOUR MAXIMUM EFFECTIVE SHOOTING DISTANCE

As Seitz quickly learned, western hunting rarely offers up a slam-dunk 10-yard shot. While I've shot several mule deer at 20 yards and less, and it is possible to get shots at this range, I often don't want to get any closer than that if I can help it. Stalking mulies

The West is tough country, so keep your setup as simple as possible to avoid in-the-field equipment problems that can wreck your hunt.

inside the 20-yard line, you'll see their radar go on red alert, often for no apparent reason. Drawing and shooting then becomes increasingly difficult. When I am personally stalking a mule deer, if I can stalk to within 30 yards, I stop and take the shot.

But getting even this close isn't always possible, thanks to a million-and-one factors that include the open country, the nature of the deer, shifting wind currents, and so on. Often the only available shot is one that can stretch to nearly the 50-yard line. For that reason, it is critical that bowhunters work hard to stretch their own maximum effective shooting distance as much as possible prior to heading West.

Can you make this 40-yard shot on a broadside buck? This is where familiarity with your equipment, a knowledge of your arrow trajectory and diligent preseason practice all come together to make—or break—your hunt.

That's not to say that you should shoot at 50-yard deer if you can't consistently make that kind of shot, or when conditions (such as a high crosswind, steep uphill or downhill angle or poor animal angle) make it a low-percentage shot. All bowhunters should stay within their own personal shooting limitations. However, the farther away you can make the shot, the better your chances of bagging a buck.

To that end, I practice at home out to 60 yards, knowing that I'll never choose to shoot at an animal farther than 50 yards away, and then only if conditions are ideal for me to make that kind of shot. I always carry a bowhunting rangefinder with me, and I use it whenever possible, when stalking a buck, and during my daily stump-shooting practice sessions. I know several bowhunters who are deadly field shots between 40 and 60 yards, and they all have one thing in common—they practice, practice, practice—and then practice some more.

Derek Phillips, a professional 3-D shooter and employee for Mathews Archery (one of the country's leading bow makers) is a superb mule deer bowhunter. "In open-country mule deer hunting, your shots will typically be 'way out there' compared to shots taken while treestand hunting," Phillips notes. "People need to know their own shooting limitations, as well as what their equipment can do. Even though I feel like I can shoot a bow with the best of them, my own personal limit is about 45 yards. But I always try to get closer. Sometimes though, you can't, so you have to be able to make that shot or you'll risk going home empty-handed."

Mule deer hunters will often find themselves shooting from their knees. Practice this type of shot religiously before heading afield.

KEEP IT SIMPLE, STUPID

The West is an ideal place for a flat-shooting bow-and-arrow setup. However, when putting together your bow, resist the urge to assemble a speed demon 3-D target-type setup that can blaze the arrows out

Bowhunters more accustomed to hunting whitetails from treestands will find that they need to modify their equipment somewhat to meet the demands of muley hunting.

there like a laser beam, but will vibrate screws and bolts loose, stress parts and need to be pampered afield. Western hunting is tough on gear, and anything that needs constant attention will eventually cause you grief. The old acronym KISS (Keep It Simple, Stupid) should be your motto.

"One thing you have to have is a bow setup that can take some field abuse," Phillips says. "You're going to bump and bang it around when spot-and-stalk hunting, so make sure your bow and its accessories are ruggedly built and can take it."

BOWS, ARROWS FOR MULE DEER

Short-axle (39 inches and shorter), lightweight compound bows that can be packed all day and easily maneuvered through the brush are ideal. Because shots at mulies can be on the long side, the flatter the trajectory you can accurately shoot, the better off you'll be. Bows that shoot their shafts at between 240 and 270 feet per second (fps) make excellent mule deer rigs. If you can squeeze a bit more raw arrow speed out of your setup, so much the better, but don't do so if the cost is poor arrow flight with broadheads.

There are many fine bows on today's market that will work very well on mule deer. Bows from companies like Mathews Archery, PSE, Hoyt USA, Bear/Jennings, Martin Archery, McPherson, Darton, Proline, Custom Shooting Systems, High Country Archery, Ben Pearson, Browning, Parker and Golden Eagle, among others, can get it done. A visit to your local archery pro shop will enable you to take the dealer's line for a "test drive" on his indoor range, where you can get a feel for how different bows shoot for you.

SuperLite aluminum, aluminum/carbon composite (A/C/C) and carbon arrow shafts are right at home when hunting mulies. Phillips shoots Easton A/C/Cs both in tournament competition and when bowhunting. He prefers small-diameter shafts for all his western hunting. "Larger diameter aluminum shafts are out for me because of the effect the wind can have on them," he says. "The A/C/Cs have better wind dynamics and

Both aluminum/carbon composite (A/C/C) and SuperLite aluminum arrow shafts are ideal choices for mule deer bowhunting. The smaller-diameter A/C/C's and pure carbon shafts will buck the wind better than fatter aluminum shafts, though.

are a little lighter than standard sized aluminum shafts, which gives me a bit flatter trajectory. Pure carbon shafts will do the same for you too. But whatever you choose, you have to use what you have a tremendous amount of confidence in. That's why I hunt with True-Flight Arrow Company's Pro Series shafts, which are easily the best finished arrow shafts I've ever shot." Pro Series shafts are bowhunting's answer to hand-loaded ammunition, made with the finest components available, a dozen raw shafts that weigh within +/- 1 grain of each other, and all of them fletched so that the high spine point of the shaft is in the same place. They're superb finished arrows.

My own current western mule deer rig is a Mathews Z-Max single-cam bow set at 72 pounds, 28$\frac{1}{2}$-inch True Flight Pro Series Beman carbon shafts and 125-grain Barrie Archery Ti-125 broadheads, which chronographs 265 fps of raw arrow speed.

You'll need a quiver to carry your arrows. While a handful of mule deer bowhunters like a hip quiver, I hate them. The arrow shafts and their fletching are constantly banging noisily on brush, and they're a hassle to use when you have to belly crawl into position—and sooner or later, you will be on your belly. A bow-attached quiver—and all bow makers offers quivers that attach snugly to their bows—keeps my shafts handy and out of the way. Sagittarius makes a great aftermarket bow quiver. If you don't like a quiver attached to your bow, a quality back quiver, like the Cat Quiver, is a great choice.

Regardless of the type of arrow shaft you choose, make sure each is straight as can be and that all components are affixed properly to ensure top-flight accuracy.

BROADHEADS

Many open-country mule deer hunters are shooting mechanical broadheads these days. Good choices include: Rocky Mountain Assassin, Revolution 100 and Gator 100; Mar-Den Vortex; New Archery Products Spitfire; Wasp Mechanic and Jak-Hammer SST; AHT Venom; Rocket Aerohead; Puckett's Bloodtrailer; Tri-Triska; and Satellite Ventilator. Of course, top-quality replaceable blade heads will get the job done too. These classic heads include: the Barrie Archery Rocky Mountain and Ti-series; New Archery Products Thunderheads; Muzzy; Sullivan Industries; Archer's Ammo; Wasp; and Satellite. Among others,

these broadheads have taken countless mulies over the last decade. The key is being able to group broadhead-tipped arrows accurately at distance. Bring some Judo and/or Bludgeon tips for stump-shooting practice.

Phillips prefers low-profile broadheads, again, because of the wind dynamics. "I used a mechanical broadhead for the first time ever in 1998, and had lots of good luck with them on mule deer," Phillips says. "They are certainly an option, but if you use them choose a top-quality one. Of course, if you tune your replaceable-blade heads to shoot like darts, they'll work great, too. But I wouldn't use one with a cutting diameter of more than $1^1/_8$ inches. This helps avoid wind problems."

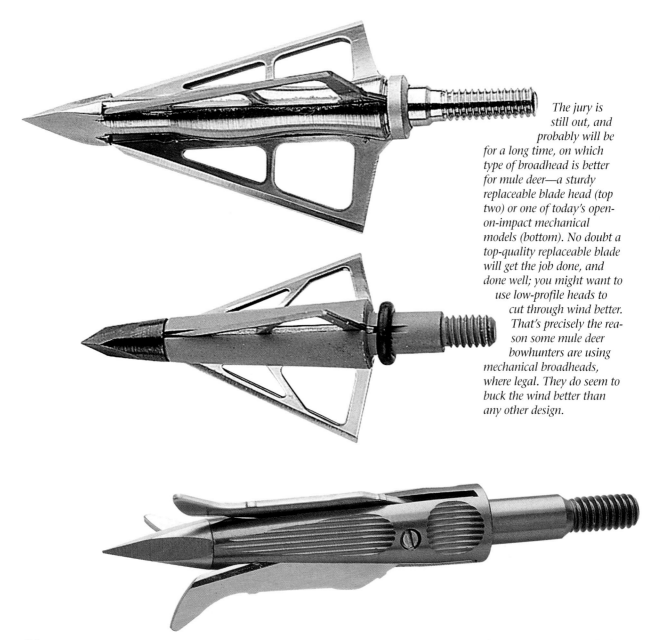

The jury is still out, and probably will be for a long time, on which type of broadhead is better for mule deer—a sturdy replaceable blade head (top two) or one of today's open-on-impact mechanical models (bottom). No doubt a top-quality replaceable blade will get the job done, and done well; you might want to use low-profile heads to cut through wind better. That's precisely the reason some mule deer bowhunters are using mechanical broadheads, where legal. They do seem to buck the wind better than any other design.

Laser rangefinder.

The most common reason bowhunters miss shots at game is that they misjudge the distance to the target. This is especially true when hunting open-country game like mule deer. For that reason, I never head afield without some type of bowhunting rangefinder.

There are two types of rangefinders—coincidence and laser. Old-style coincidence rangefinders use the principle of triangulation to tell you the distance. Ranging, Inc., makes the most common type. They're relatively inexpensive, rugged and work fairly well. However, nothing beats the new generation of laser rangefinders. Powered by a single 9V battery, with a single push of a button these units can tell you, within +/- 1 yard, the distance to your target whether it's 15 yards away or farther than you could possibly shoot. At various times I've used the Bushnell Yardage Pro 400 and Yardage Pro Compact 600 (my favorite for bowhunting) and Brunton Laser 70, with excellent results. Swarovski and Leica make superb units costing thousands

of dollars, if you've got that much money to spend. I wear my Bushnell units around my neck using a Crooked Horn Outfitters Slide and Flex Binocular System, which keeps it handy for instant use and also keeps my clothing tight to my chest and off my bow string.

Laser rangefinders will set you back a couple hundred bucks, but are, in my opinion, an essential tool for the mule deer bowhunter. You can read more about them later in this chapter.

Coincidence rangefinder.

Shooting Uphill & Downhill

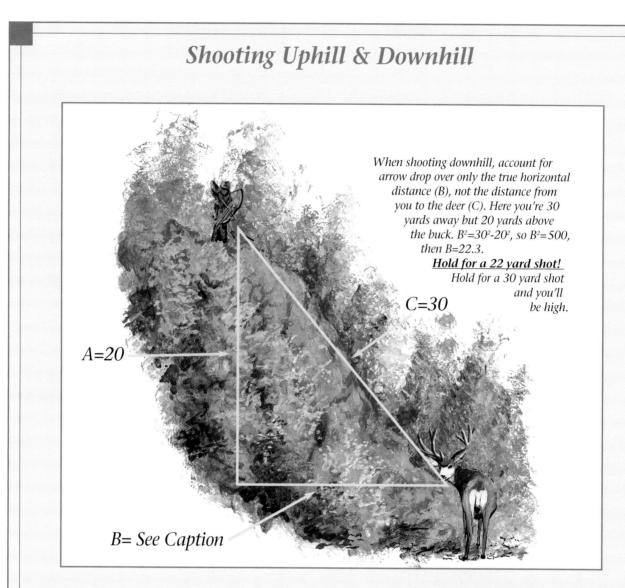

When shooting downhill, account for arrow drop over only the true horizontal distance (B), not the distance from you to the deer (C). Here you're 30 yards away but 20 yards above the buck. $B^2=30^2-20^2$, so $B^2=500$, then $B=22.3$.

<u>Hold for a 22 yard shot!</u>
Hold for a 30 yard shot and you'll be high.

C=30

A=20

B= See Caption

Because archers often stalk mule deer from above, it is important to understand arrow trajectory on steep downhill angles. The physics of gravity control arrow flight. Gravity exerts its influence on the arrow only on the horizontal flight of the arrow. Here's how that affects uphill and downhill shooting.

When you shoot horizontally at a target 50 yards away, gravity exerts its influence on the arrow for the full 50 yards, and the arrow follows a trajectory you've come to understand through routine practice. However, when you shoot either uphill or, more commonly in muley hunting, downhill, the horizontal distance will be less than the actual distance you are standing from the deer. For example, if you're standing 50 yards

from the deer and 25 yards above him, the actual linear distance to the deer is only roughly 43.3 yards. Thus, if you use your rangefinder and get a 50 yard reading and use your 50-yard sight pin, your arrow will hit high, possibly going over the deer's back. Instead you need to aim for 43 yards.

With practice you'll learn to "eyeball" these changes. If you want to get technical, it's all a geometry axiom called the Pythagorean theorem, which states that on any triangle with a right angle, A squared plus B squared = C squared, if A is the vertical height you are above the deer, B is the true horizontal distance, and C is the longest distance (see diagram). Here's one example. My rangefinder tells me it's 50 yards to the deer, and I estimate I am 25 yards above the deer.

According to the Pythagorean theorem, B squared would = C squared minus A squared, or 2,500 minus 625, or 1,875. The square root of 1,875 is roughly 43.3, which means the linear distance to the deer—the distance I need to aim for—is 43 yards.

Another example, using different distances, is with the diagram at left.

You won't go through all this math and rigamarole with your heart pounding and a nice mule deer buck browsing down the slope from you. But smart mule deer hunters practice shooting at life-sized animal targets before their hunt to help them understand how their arrows fly downhill at various distances. This is one math test you can't afford to fail.

When shooting up or downhill, compensate before you aim and release.

The key feature of any bow sight used for mule deer hunting is ruggedness. It must be able to take a pounding without breaking, or it will be rendered useless in no time.

BOW SIGHTS

There are two things a bow sight needs to be for all western bowhunting: rugged and dependable. Your sight will take some knocks, and if that abuse damages it, you're history. Regardless of the type of sight you choose—pin, crosshair or movable-pin-type sights are the most popular—make sure it is built tough.

In the early days, bow sights featured simple metal pins. These are great when it's bright outside, but in dim light you can't see them well enough to make the shot. For that reason, bright sight pins are a big advantage in all shooting situations. The new generation of fiber-optic sight pins are the way to go, and what I use for virtually all of my bowhunting. Phillips is also a believer in fiber-optic sight pins. "I love them, even in open country, especially at dawn and dusk, and especially on cloudy, overcast days," he says.

I also prefer using a peep sight, but that's a personal thing. A peep sight helps you sight your bow like a rifle, providing a rear aperture that makes shooting more accurately—especially at longer distances—easier than shooting without one.

BLACKPOWDER BUCKS

*I*t was cold and rainy that November week, with snow dusting the upper ridges. That didn't deter my hunting buddy, Jim Matthews, and me though. We had non-resident tags for one of Utah's first-ever black-powder-only mule deer hunts, and we were in an area where there were some dandies.

We'd chosen to hunt the blackpowder season for the same reason I seriously rediscovered bowhunting several years earlier—no tags were issued for rifle hunters during the rut, but if you hunted with a "primitive weapon," like a muzzleloader, you could hunt rutting bucks. We were as excited as all get out.

Jim and I never did shoot a deer that trip, even though we saw several good bucks moving in and out of the thick brush. It was good hunting, but getting close enough to shoot was a problem. We were hunting with replicas of percussion Hawken rifles we'd built from kits, which were accurate enough with open sights to maybe 75 yards on a good day. We also discovered that if you let your Pyrodex get wet, it would turn into a rock-hard substance that reminded me a lot of Play-Doh, that clay stuff we played with as kids that was gooey and workable when moist but, when dry, took on the consistency of concrete. When that happened, you had to pull your bullet and literally chip the charge out of the barrel.

Be that as it may, I was hooked. Soon I was applying for muzzleloader-only tags around the West as they became available, and regularly hunted mule deer and elk in several states. With an excited eye, I've seen the technology in rifles and accessories evolve. Today, muzzleloading mule deer hunters have the finest equipment ever. It's easy to travel "back to the future" and become a successful muzzleloader mule deer hunter.

MODERN "HUNTERS" VS. OLD-TIME "TRADITIONALISTS"

In the 1960s and '70s, when states first began offering a few special muzzleloader-only seasons, hunters who chose muzzleloaders were more concerned with nostalgia, hoping to step back in time and hunt with the tools of the old trappers and pioneers. At the same time in many parts of the country deer numbers—especially eastern whitetails—were nothing like they are today. With few antlerless seasons, the chances of success on any hunting trip were not especially good, and many blackpowder hunters of that era thought, "What the heck, I'd just as soon go home empty-handed hunting with a tool that brings back memories and helps me live out my wilderness fantasies." State wildlife managers also were more concerned with providing increased hunter opportunity while not significantly increasing the overall deer harvest. For that reason the muzzleloader seasons were quite restrictive.

The muzzleloading hunters of today are, for the most part, deer hunters more concerned with the chance to put a tag on an animal during one of the special muzzleloader-only seasons—especially seasons held during the rut—than with nostalgic ties to yesterday. Most probably have never even read The Leatherstocking Tales, or seen the old Daniel Boone and Davy Crockett TV shows that inspired many more traditional muzzleloader shooters. And while some states restrict the use of certain types of muzzleloaders during their blackpowder seasons, the general public, for the most part, is more concerned with performance than nostalgia: Muzzleloaders just let you get out hunting more!

BLACKPOWDER RIFLES

Today you have two choices of rifle style: exposed-hammer and in-line.

Exposed-hammer rifles are of the classic design, with a hammer you thumb back to cock before firing. They are still very popular, and today there are some sidehammer rifles available that rival the more modern in-line style in performance and accuracy.

However, in-line rifles are truly the "back to the future" of muzzleloading. "In-line" refers to the muzzleloader's ignition system, which places the rifle's nipple and percussion cap in a straight line with the

More and more muley hunters are taking afield with muzzleloaders these days. And why not? Many states are offering special muzzleloader-only seasons held during the rut, when the odds of finding a buck with over-sized headgear are best.

barrel and powder charge. No longer does the spark have to make a sharp turn to find the powder, which has improved the reliability of the ignition so much that the hangfires and misfires that so often plagued

Traditional flintlock or percussion, or modern in-line muzzleloader? It all boils down to an individual choice, and what pleases you as a hunter.

elk season in the late '70s and early '80s. Being new to the blackpowder game, they soon found—as many of us did—they had trouble making their reproduction percussion rifles go off when they wanted, if they could even haul the long-barreled 9-pound guns up and down the mountains. They took their troubles to Knight, who had a small shop in the garage of the family farm and no muzzleloading experience. Without any preconceived notions, he designed a hunting rifle that just happened to be a muzzleloader. In his eye, hunting rifles had round 22-inch barrels (not 3-foot octagon tubes), weighed less than 8 pounds and used a practical in-line ignition design.

Knight made his first in-line rifle in 1983. In 1985 he introduced the Knight MK-85, which set the tone for both the industry and the hunters it served. The Modern Muzzleloading, Inc., MK-85 had modern rifle features, including receivers drilled and tapped for scope mounts and an adjustable trigger, plus a removable breech plug that greatly simplified cleaning and permitted hunters to push an unfired charge out the breech at day's end, instead of having to either pull the ball or bullet out of the barrel or fire the rifle, which meant a half-hour's cleaning session. Other makers like White, Thompson/Center and CVA soon jumped on the bandwagon. Today there is a raft of additional companies, like Traditions, Gonic Arms, Markesbery Muzzleloaders, Navy Arms, Dixie Gun Works and Austen & Halleck offering top-quality in-line muzzleloaders. And many names most of us associate with centerfire rifles—Remington, Ruger and Marlin—are in the game too.

IN-LINE PERFORMANCE

Despite all the hoopla, in-lines are still muzzleloading blackpowder firearms. To hear many of their detractors, you'd think they provide the ballistic performance of some new souped up centerfire magnum round. Not so. However, they do provide better ballistic performance than the front stuffers of old.

more traditional percussion rifles are as rare as four-leaf clovers.

Most people don't realize that the in-line design is not a true modern development, but rather, an improvement on a basic design that dates back to 1700s-era flintlocks. Theory has it that a lack of springs strong enough to drive the in-line hammers forward fast enough probably kept this design from supplanting sidehammer firearms. And while in the 1970s and '80s there were a few in-lines around, they never really did catch on with hunters and shooters.

Presto! Along came Tony Knight, a gunsmith from Lancaster, Missouri. Knight had customers who traveled to Colorado to hunt the state's muzzleloader-only

For example, my standard deer hunting load for several of the .50 caliber in-lines I've hunted with (.50 caliber is by far the most popular caliber sold today, followed by .54 caliber) produces about 1,475 foot-pounds (fp) of energy at the muzzle, and retains 1,100 fp at 100 yards when using a saboted conical bullet weighing in the 240- to 260-grain class and 100-grain equivalent of Pyrodex Select or two Pyrodex Pellets. I can get a bit more energy, but lose a bit of trajectory, by going up to a 300-grain bullet. Still, if I zero these rifles to print between two and three inches high at 100 yards—the same way I sight in most of my centerfire rifles—the bullet will strike three or four inches low at 150 yards. Group size isn't satisfactory to me if I can't produce three-shot, two-inch clusters at 100 yards.

However, many in-lines can outshine this performance. New rifles from Modern Muzzleloading (Knight), Thompson/Center and Traditions are built to accept three 50-grain Pyrodex Pellets. When loaded with a

250-grain sabot-encased bullet, they can produce muzzle velocities of 2,100 fps or more. Gonic Arms has touted its Magnum Muzzleloader as being able to produce a startling 3,000 fp of energy at the muzzle and M.O.A. (1-inch group at 100 yards) accuracy right out of the box.

Noted Outdoor Life gun writer Jim Carmichael once did an extensive test on in-line ballistics using four different scoped in-line .50 caliber rifles—Knight Hawk MK-85, Remington Model 700 MLS, T/C Firehawk and White Lightning, plus a Big Bore Express Alexander Henry Style Caplock rifle—shooting three-shot groups at 100 yards using 11 different bullets and a 90-grain equivalent charge of Pyrodex RS Select propellant—to test accuracy and muzzle velocity. Carmichael's test showed what many of us have discovered doing similar range work—that you can achieve consistent 100-yard groups of less than two inches with the right bullet-and-charge combination from most quality production in-line rifles.

Tony Knight, pioneer of the modern in-line muzzleloader, with a good muley in velvet. Overleaf: No matter what type of muzzle-loader you carry afield, it may be one of your best chances to meet up with a big buck like this one ... either early in the season before he hasn't seen any hunting pressure all summer, or late during the rut when he's interested in the does.

Choose Your Weapon

A synthetic-stocked, scoped in-line muzzleloader is a highly accurate, extremely dependable hunting rifle that can cleanly take mule deer out to the 200-yard line. Not all states permit scope sights to be used, however.

SIGHTING SYSTEMS

Most modern muzzleloaders come with adjustable iron sights. However, many experienced shooters upgrade their sighting systems. Fiber-optic sights are a superb choice for hunting with open sights. Some rifle makers offer them as standard fare, and you can also get them as an aftermarket replacement part; both Williams Gun Sight Company and TruGlo make good ones. Some hunters replace their factory open sights with a peep sight like Thompson/Center's Tang Peep Sight.

Where legal, many muzzleloaders choose to scope their rifles. (Scopes are not legal in every state, so be sure to check regulations first.) Some optics manufacturers like Burris, Bushnell, Leupold, Redfield and Simmons sell scopes designed specifically for modern muzzleloaders. However, many in-line shooters equip their rifles with the same top-quality variable rifle scope they use on their centerfire rifles.

LOADING UP

While the classic patched round ball is still shot by some, where legal most muzzleloading mule deer

hunters use either conical bullets or sabot-encased conicals. (See sidebar.) Many different companies offer quality muzzleloading bullets today, including well-known blackpowder rifle makers like Thompson/Center, CVA, Traditions, Knight Rifles and Remington, as well as specialists like Buffalo Bullet Co., Muzzleload Magnum Products (MMP), Precision

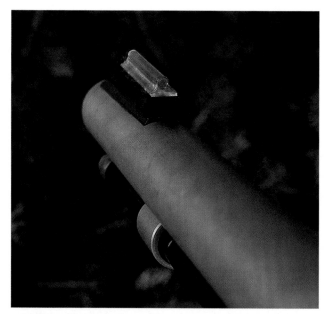

Adding a fiber optic front sight to an open sighting system will help you make an accurate shot on the cusp of daylight, when bucks are most active.

These days, most muzzleloaders choose to hunt with some type of conical, or sabot-encased conical, bullet. These bullets provide performance far superior to traditional round-ball loads.

Rifle Bullets, Northern Precision, Parker Productions, Black Belt Bullets from Big Bore Express and Game Buster Bullets, and well-known and easily recognizable centerfire ammunition and bullet makers like Hornady, Barnes, Nosler, Swift Bullet Co. and Lyman.

There are two basic propellant types—old-style blackpowder and Hodgdon's Pyrodex, available in both traditional granulated and Pyrodex Pellets forms. Blackpowder—GOEX and Elephant Black Powder are the most popular—is more susceptible to problems with moisture, but many hunters like it because it provides very uniform velocities and accuracy. Pyrodex is less susceptible to moisture troubles (although you have to keep it dry too, as we discovered years ago in Utah), and it isn't quite as corrosive. Pellets feature preformed and premeasured charges that make loading quick and easy in the field. They work great.

ESSENTIAL ACCESSORIES

Blackpowder rifles must be meticulously cleaned after each shooting session to avoid rust and corrosion. Cleaning supplies like ramrods and attachments, patches and cleaning solvents are often packaged in kit form, or they can be purchased separately. These and other items—like powder measures, powder

A Book Muzzleloader Buck

For the first time in two weeks it was raining like a bull doing his business on the proverbial flat rock. Usually when deer hunting, that's bad news. In southwestern Oregon blacktail country, though, that's what the doctor ordered. Medford Guide Doug Gattis told me the deer always move much better when it's raining than when it's dry.

"Right," I remember thinking. "They have to tell you *something* when the day is going to be a bust." After all, who wants to hunt with a muzzleloader in the cold November rain?

An hour into the morning I saw what Gattis meant. The biggest blacktail buck I've seen in 25 years of seriously chasing them was nosing a doe along, oblivious to our presence. In the dim gray light the after-market fiber-optic sight I'd added to my Thompson/Center System 1 .50-caliber in-line rifle stood out like a beacon, and the 60-yard shot was a short one. The 250-grain Nosler Partition-HG Hunting Sabot, pushed along by a

pair of 50-grain Pyrodex Pellets, did the job superbly. The buck's symmetrical antlers later scored an official 154$^1/_8$ Boone and Crockett points, which would place him Number 85 in the all-time B&C record book. I didn't start shaking until it was all over.

The only reason I was able to hunt a buck of this caliber was by choosing a muzzleloader-only season. Shouldn't you be applying for those tags too?

Choose Your Weapon

Conical vs. Sabot Bullets

Conical bullets are the choice of most modern muzzleloading hunters. However, where legal, smart muzzleloaders are using conicals encased in a plastic "sabot."

The sabot is a plastic wad, like those found in modern shotshells, that encases the bullet tightly in the barrel. This does three things. First, it prevents gas from escaping around the bullet, maximizing velocity. Second, it allows you to use a smaller-caliber bullet than the bore size, meaning a lighter, and therefore, faster bullet. And third, it helps promote maximum accuracy. The military learned all of this decades ago; this is one reason they use nothing but sabot-encased projectiles in tank cannons. Sabots also help prevent bore fouling by keeping the lead or copper of the bullet from touching the barrel, where it will leave hard-to-remove deposits. You'll also find them easier to load.

When you want maximum bullet weight—as in elk hunting with a .50 caliber rifle, for example—using a non-sabot-encased bullet may make sense. But for mule deer hunting, using sabots makes you a more efficient shooter.

flasks, speed loaders, percussion caps, cappers, possible bags and pouches and other accessories—are offered by many major gun makers and also by well-known aftermarket accessory manufacturers like Uncle Mike's and Bridgers Best. One excellent accessory item is the Dry Fire Breech Protector, a simply designed product that keeps moisture out of the breech area of many models of in-line muzzleloaders. Another is the Traditions EZ Unloader, which uses a blast of compressed air at the breech end to push powder and projectile down and out the barrel when unloading at day's end.

Blackpowder hunters need lots of specialized accessories, including percussion caps, a capper, bullet starter, nipple wrench, powder flask and powder measure, among others. Be sure to work up an accurate hunting load well before opening day.

HANDGUNS

S ome mule deer hunters like to pursue big bucks with handguns. It's a real challenge, especially since handgunners have no separate special season when they have the deer all to themselves, like archers and muzzleloaders.

Handgun hunters generally choose between two pistol types—revolvers and single-shot specialty pistols.

REVOLVERS

Revolver hunters have the choice of some of the finest handguns ever made. Popular calibers include the .41 magnum—generally considered the minimum revolver caliber for big-game hunting—.44 magnum and the powerful .454 Casull. Friends who can handle the Casull's power are crack shots at 100 to 125 yards with their scoped pistols, while those hunting with the .41 and .44 magnums try to keep their shots inside 100 yards.

Revolver hunters have been blessed in recent years by the development of ammunition and bullets designed expressly for big game hunting. These jacketed bullets penetrate deeply, yet expand rapidly once inside the chest cavity, at revolver velocities. Winchester, Federal and Remington make excellent ammo that's deadly on mule deer.

SINGLE-SHOT PISTOLS

Handgun hunting got a big boost when the late Bob Milek, a friend and colleague with whom I worked while on staff at *Petersen's Hunting* magazine, worked together with Dick Dietz of Remington and stock maker Steve Herrett, and developed the single-shot specialty pistol in the early 1980s. His love of handgun hunting on the open plains near his Wyoming home opened a new world of hunting and shooting to thousands of sportsmen.

Single-shot specialty pistols feature crisp triggers, well-built stocks, and accurate barrels between 10 and 16 inches long. There are two actions types: break-open, popularized by the Thompson/Center Contender and Encore; and bolt-action, developed by Milek, Dietz and Herrett and popularized by the Remington XP-100. Today there are others of this type, notably the Savage Striker. Some, like the modern XP-100, have blind magazines. Many have synthetic stocks.

These pistols must be fired from a solid rest to achieve accurate bullet flight, but the best of them can group five shots inside a half-dollar at 100 yards all day long. They are chambered for some of the best deer hunting cartridges ever, including the 7mm-08 Rem., .308 and .30-06, as well as a host of wildcat cartridges designed to give near rifle performance. The most popular line of wildcat cartridges was designed by well-known handgun hunter, J.D. Jones. In all cases, they can be loaded with spitzer-type hunting bullets designed to perform exactly like those found in centerfire rifle ammunition on deer-sized game. In some cases, the exact same ammunition can be used.

Single-shot specialty pistols are fun to shoot and, in the hands of a skilled shooter, as deadly on mule deer as any firearm.

SCOPES & ACCESSORIES

Many revolver and most single-shot pistol hunters scope their handguns. There are several top-quality scopes, in both fixed- and variable-power versions, designed expressly for this purpose, as well as superb scope mounts for them. Pistol scopes must have a longer eye relief than rifle scopes.

Companies like Michael's of Oregon offer excellent shoulder holsters for both revolver and single-shot pistols hunters. I've seen lightweight Harris bipods attached to the forend of some single-shot pistols, and many hunters carry shooting sticks (my favorites are those from Stoney Point Products) to help achieve a solid rest in the field. And there are also reloading dies, brass and components readily available, whether you choose standard or wildcat cartridges.

Handgun hunting is not for everyone, but I enjoy it immensely. If you like shooting as much as you do hunting, you'll find it a most pleasurable way to take the mule deer challenge.

The handgunning challenge involves getting closer to your quarry: within 100 yards, preferably 50 or less. Any legal mule deer is a trophy under these circumstances!

LASER RANGEFINDERS: DON'T LEAVE HOME WITHOUT ONE

ule deer hunters can find good shots from a few yards to "way out there," depending on the country, conditions and the type of weapons they use. Whether I'm hunting with my bow, muzzleloader, or custom .300 Win. Mag., I've found that a laser rangefinder is both fun and helpful in making the shot at the extreme end of the maximum effective range of my weapon.

There are two kinds of rangefinders—coincidence and laser. Coincidence units, popularized by Ranging, Inc., work on the principle of triangulation. They have two windows and a system of prisims and lenses that produce the two images you see when you look through the viewfinder. You simply turn a precalibrated dial, stopping when the two images coincide and become one, then read the distance off the dial. With a bit of practice, these types of units are quite accurate. Ranging's 1000 is a 1,000-yard model of this type. Coincidence rangefinders are relatively inexpensive, but they can be tricky to use, especially at long distance.

That's why the laser rangefinder is the way to go. Laser units function by sending out a beam of light—a laser beam—that is reflected off the target object. The amount of time it takes for the beam to go out and return to the rangefinder unit is mathematically translated by the unit into the precise distance from the unit to the target. Today's laser rangefinders are precise to within plus or minus one or two yards at their advertised distances. They're compact, and can either be worn around the neck with a strap or carried in a soft belt pouch. They work on a standard 9V battery that will give hundreds of "shots" before wearing down. They can also take a fair amount of field abuse and keep on ticking.

The best units I've used are from Bushnell, including their Yardage Pro 400, Yardage Pro 800, and Yardage Pro Compact 600 and 1000. I've taken these units into weather ranging from 100°F to minus 50°F without a problem. The Brunton 70 is a 70-yard unit that works well for bowhunting. Companies like Swarovski and Leica make outstanding combination binocular/rangefinder units costing several thousand dollars. The others cost from around $200 to $300.

The Bushnell Compact 600 is excellent for bowhunting and when I'm carrying either my muzzleloader or handgun. But I prefer the Compact 1000 when I'm rifle hunting. I use them two ways. When time and conditions permit, I'll try to take a reading on an animal I'm hoping to shoot. I also use them to take readings throughout the day, which helps me learn to "eyeball" the often-deceptive distance on open plains, across deep, wide canyons and from high vantage points to the valley below. Both uses are very helpful.

Chapter 3

MULE DEER GEAR

A good buddy and I were sitting on top of a high ridge overlooking the pinion/juniper country of Arizona's Kaibab Plateau. We'd been busting our behinds for a week and had yet to glass up a really good buck. And we were getting tired. The long hours, little sleep and mile after mile of climbing and hiking were starting to take their toll.

As he dug into his pack for some lunch, my friend got frustrated. "I can't find anything is this mess," he grumbled, then dumped everything on the ground. He had more "stuff" than most hunting shops. Looking at that pile it was obvious why he was getting tired—he was lugging around 25 pounds of stuff we wouldn't need in a million years!

"Remember when we were in high school?" he asked. "All we did then was stick a book of matches in our pocket, grab our rifles and skinning knives and go hunting."

No doubt about it—modern deer hunters like their "stuff." And we've been conditioned by both manufacturers and the media to believe that we cannot hunt successfully without a bag full of gadgets, and we can't safely navigate the wilderness without whiz-bang electronics. Plus it's all so easy to get with mail-order catalogs and the Internet thrust upon us.

If there's one thing I've learned after nearly 30 years of mule deer hunting, it's this—while we need the right stuff in the field, and much of today's high-tech equipment and clothing is so much better than the gear we had decades ago—there can be too much of a good thing when it comes to packing around all sorts of gadgets and gizmos up, down and all around the wide-open spaces of the West. We need to choose our equipment wisely, carefully balancing between what we'd like to have with us, and what we really need to be comfortable, safe and successful buck hunters.

How do you know what you really need and don't need to be the best mule deer hunter you can be? Read on and let me help you sort it all out ...

SEEING IS BELIEVING

Above and beyond all else, serious mule deer hunting is a game of glassing. Consistently successful muley hunters learn that the best way to find the buck they want is to find a good vantage point, plop down and glass for hours. They also know that glassing into dark, shaded areas, thick cover and at the cusp of daylight are where they are most likely to locate deer. (More on this in chapter 4, "How to Hunt Mule Deer.")

To that end, more important than just about any other equipment choice—including everything from your rifle or bow to your boots—selecting the right pair of binoculars is the most important decision you'll ever make. How so? First, because unless you

can find and identify deer under the full spectrum of conditions, you can't shoot one. It's that simple. Second, good binoculars won't give you eyestrain and the accompanying headache. You'll feel better and hunt longer and harder.

"Okay," you think, "I need a new pair of binoculars," and the search begins. Soon you are so confused by technical terms and overwhelmed by the price spectrum you don't know what to do. How do you sort all this out?

When shopping for new binoculars or a new spotting scope, remember only one word: quality. Buying the best binoculars you can afford is a lifetime investment in increased hunting success. I've never heard a

Need a new pair of binoculars? Buy the very best you can afford. The price may hurt at first, but your optics will give you a lifetime of high-quality performance.

discouraging word from hunters who carry binoculars from Zeiss, Swarovski, Bausch & Lomb or Leica, which also happen to be the most expensive. Simmons, Nikon, Burris, Fujinon, Pentax, Leupold, Swift and Steiner also make good binoculars that cost less money. Advanced mule deer hunters also know that even though they weigh more, full-sized binoculars with relatively large objective lenses are easier to hold steady, and their larger lenses allow hunters to see better in dim dawn and dusk light, when game is most active. That's why they avoid compact binoculars like the plague.

KEY HUNTING BINOCULAR FEATURES

Top-of-the-line hunting binoculars include several key features that you can use as your benchmark when comparing brands "A" and "B."

Light-Gathering Ability: In hunting situations, the more ability binoculars have to gather and utilize available light, the better. This is critical very early and late in the day, when game is most active. Generally speaking, the larger the objective lens, the more light is transmitted to your eye. For example, 10x50 binocu-

lars deliver more light than a 10x28. To compare binoculars on an even scale, simply divide the size of the objective lens by the magnification to get the "twilight factor." For example, 10x50 binoculars have a twilight factor of 5.0, while 8x30s have a twilight factor of 3.75; under dim-light conditions, you'll see better with the 10x50s.

The Importance of Coatings: Light tends to reflect off glass, and by the time it bounces off the multiple surfaces of a modern day pair of binoculars, as much as half the light that initially entered the system may have bounced back out. (There are many more lenses and glass surfaces inside a pair of binoculars than just the objective and ocular lenses.) This can severely reduce the brightness and image quality if it weren't for the chemical coatings on the lenses designed to reduce reflection. All quality binoculars have at least some coatings, but do not necessarily have a coating on all internal surfaces. Top-of-the-line binoculars have high-tech coatings on all lens surfaces, a big reason high-end binoculars cost so much.

Clarity: You must be able to see distant objects clearly, with no eyestrain. If objects appear blurry, or your eyes feel tired after looking through the binoculars, they aren't the ones for you.

Waterproof, Fogproof: Hunting binoculars should be guaranteed 100 percent waterproof and fogproof. Years ago, this was found only in the most expensive glasses, but today most manufacturers guarantee their products from the mid-price point range on up. Avoid products without this assurance.

Full-sized binoculars utilize more light than compact models, making it much easier to spot deer as they move at dawn and dusk, their most active periods.

More mule deer hunters carry full-sized 10X binoculars afield than any other size, with 8X the second most popular choice.

HOW MUCH POWER IS TOO MUCH?

Decades ago, the experts' mantra was that low-power binoculars in the 6X to 7X range was the ideal choice. Yet today, the biggest sellers are 10X binoculars. There are a couple of reasons for this. First, the quality of today's binoculars is so much better than those of a generation ago that seeing clearly through a pair of higher-power binoculars today is a given. Second, most of today's hunters ply their trade from a static position, watching from treestands, shooting houses or ground blinds for whitetails ... or glassing from high on a mountain ridge for mule deer. From a rock-solid, stationary position, today's quality 10X binoculars will give you a crisp, clean and steady look at game, and the higher magnification makes spotting and evaluating far-away mule deer much easier.

However, lower-power binoculars have their place

too. When still-hunting or sitting a stand in tight cover, for example, lower-power binoculars with a wider field of view are a definite advantage. Generally, for mule deer hunting the minimum power to consider is 8X, with 10X my own preferred "all-around" choice.

SHOPPING FOR NEW HUNTING BINOCULARS

Unless you shop at a camera store or serious hunting shop with an experienced staff, you'll get little help when trying to select a new pair of binoculars. The best way is to compare as many brands as possible side by side outside the store.

"Shop at a store with a good selection so you can make valid comparisons," says Barbara Mellman, head of public relations for Bushnell and Bausch & Lomb binoculars for more than 20 years. "Call the dealer up and tell them you're seriously shopping, and ask if you can come over and test several binoculars outside in a 'real world' environment. Shopping at sunset is the best time, or on a cloudy or rainy day, so you can compare in dim light."

Take several different makes and models to a shaded area, and sit down. It's best not to look over pavement because heat distortion can be a problem; looking over grass is better. Choose a distant object to focus on, like a tree limb outlined against the sky 100 yards away. Does it appear crisp and sharp, or is it soft? Next, spend a little time looking around, concentrating on small, complex shapes at various distances. My favorite test is to look into dark, shaded areas. If I can't see into them well, I'm not happy.

When shopping for new binoculars, take several different makes and models outside the store and try them out, preferably in dim light. That's the best way to find a pair you really like.

Don't kid yourself. You need binoculars—good ones—to find a mule deer in all this country. Those glasses shouldn't reside in your daypack, either. Use them. Often.

Just as important, when you take the binoculars away from your eyes, can you see perfectly without the feeling that your eyes are trying hard to refocus themselves? If so, there might be a problem with the binocular's collimation. One of the most difficult tasks in binocular manufacturing is perfectly aligning both lenses so that you are looking in exactly the same direction with both eyes. Using binoculars with faulty collimation leads to severe eyestrain.

"Select different brands of the power and objective lens size you have decided on," Mellman says. "Then find out how comfortably they fit in your hand. Outside, look into dark areas or corners to get a feeling for the relative brightness of each. Then weigh in other factors, including brightness, clarity, comfort, exterior comfort of holding and carrying them, waterproofness and the manufacturer's reputation and warranty program. The last thing you should consider, though, is price. When buying binoculars, you really do get what you pay for."

HOW MUCH WILL THEY COST?

Generally speaking, the old saying, "You get what you pay for," is never truer than when shopping for hunting binoculars. Making high-quality binoculars requires precision engineering, manufacturing to extreme tolerances and the use of sophisticated coatings on virtually all glass surfaces. This all costs money.

You can spend as little or as much as you want. As of this writing, in one of the major hunting catalogs you could order 10x42 or 10x50 porro prism binoculars for as little as $74.99 or as much as $1,299. Mid-range prices range from $229 to $469.

I look at shopping for hunting binoculars as a lifetime investment. If I plan on using these glasses for the next 20 years, spending $1,000 or more doesn't seem like so much when I think about the cost per year of use. And remember, the price of top-end binoculars isn't going down. For example, I bought a pair of Zeiss 10x40 binoculars almost 15 years ago for a little more than $300, which was the price of a quality hunting rifle in those days. Today those same glasses cost nearly $1,000. It was one of the best investments I've ever made.

Nevertheless, you can get good binoculars for less money—if you do your research and test/compare extensively.

WHAT DO I USE?

I learned long ago that there is no one pair of binoculars that is perfect for every hunting situation.

A sturdy tripod will steady both a spotting scope and a pair of binoculars, helping you spot more deer at extended ranges. Make sure your tripod will extend high enough so it will reach over tall brush.

For that reason I have two pairs that get the most use, depending on the type of hunting I'm doing. In addition, I have a pair of "specialty" binoculars I use for specialized hunting.

I use my 10x42 pair the most. They are excellent for general spot-and-stalk hunting for mule deer, as well as sitting in stands over large fields. When bowhunting tight cover, or still-hunting through dark timber, my 7x35s are used the most. They give me all the magnification I need, gather lots of light and provide a wide field of view.

Like many western hunters, I've found that the farther I can see, the better my chances. To that end, many years ago my friend DuWane Adams, a superb mule and Coues' deer guide from Arizona, pioneered the use of oversized, tripod-mounted binoculars for spotting bucks over vast distances. DuWane began using a pair of 15x60 Zeiss binoculars for this task and soon was able to "pick up" deer at distances of a mile or more.

Spotting Scopes

Serious muley hunters pack a top-quality spotting scope for evaluating antlers at long range. A good spotter can save you hours of time and miles of walking and should be a standard part of your equipment.

Spotters have to gather enough light so you can see in dim light, and must be light enough to pack up the mountain, rugged enough to take some field abuse and powerful enough to permit antler evaluation at a mile or more. I prefer variable-power spotting scopes, with eyepieces in the 15-45X and 20-60X class. For many years I carried a Bausch & Lomb Elite 15-45X spotter with 60mm objective lens, as well as their 20-60X model with 70mm objective lens. These scopes have excellent optics and can really take a pounding in the field. I've also used spotting scopes from Leupold, Redfield, Burris, Simmons, Fujinon and Nikon with good results. Expect to pay $450 to $700 for a good spotting scope of this type. Leica and Swarovski make Cadillac-quality spotting scopes,

but they cost well over $1,000 and are relatively big and bulky.

You need a good tripod with a spotting scope. I've yet to find a manufacturer that provides a satisfactory one with the scope. Instead, buy a lightweight camera tripod. Get one that extends high enough so that you can sit—not lie down—comfortably behind it without craning your neck. They'll weigh maybe a pound and cost about $50.

Optical Support

One of the most overlooked keys to glassing effectively is supporting your binoculars. This does two things. First, it steadies your glasses a million times better than using just your arms. And second, it eliminates user fatigue, which in turn causes the binoculars to wobble and shake. Standing up and glassing is useless for all but a quick look at a suspicious object. Sitting or lying prone is much better. Resting the glasses on a log or rock will help. Some western hunters sit behind their pack frames and rest their binoculars over the top bar. Advanced glassers who scan lots of country for long periods of time, or who use binoculars of 10X or more, often use a lightweight camera tripod fitted with a special adapter designed to secure their binoculars on top. This is Cadillac glassing. Tripod/binocular adapters that screw the binoculars solidly onto the tripod, are available at many camera shops. Bass Pro Shops also sell a Binocular Tripod Mount featuring a plastic base and system of Velcro straps.

You'll also need a comfortable neck strap. Forget the thin nylon straps that come with your binoculars from the factory. They'll cut your neck and make even smallish binoculars feel as heavy as bricks by day's end. A better choice is a wide neoprene strap like the QD Deluxe Bino Strap from Butler Creek of Belgrade, Montana, or Vero Vellini. These straps actually "give" a little with each step, cushioning the shock, and help distribute the weight of the glass over a wide area. They're a great product.

Many hunters use what I call a "binocular bra." These are after-market products that combine a comfortable neck strap with a system that holds the binoculars tight to your chest, yet permits you to easily and quickly raise and use them. The best two I've used are the Crooked Creek Slide & Flex Bino System and the Bino Buddy. I like these products a lot.

I was fortunate enough to learn this from DuWane early on, and soon was finding my own bucks through a pair of my own 15x60s. (Today you can also find 20x80 binoculars that serve the same function.) I still use these glasses a lot today, especially in the open country of the Southwest, as well as when glassing across vast mountain canyons. Often I'll pack both my 15x60s and 10x42s, using both in the same day. I hate to carry extra weight in my hunting pack, but am so dependent on being able to "glass 'em up" that I almost feel naked without them.

One final thought. In hunting, you spend a lot more time looking for game than actually shooting at it. Thus, you'll spend many more hours looking through your binoculars than actually pulling the trigger. Despite this, most hunters spend much more time and money on their selection of firearms and bows than they do on their binoculars. The more time you experience in the field, the more you realize that the most important tool you carry is not necessarily your weapon, but your eyes. And if your eyes are strained, you will get headaches and lose your desire to hunt hard.

Shop hard for your next pair of binoculars, and buy the very best you can afford. You'll never regret it.

BACKPACK BASICS

rowing up near California's magnificent Sierra Nevada Mountains, I learned a lot about back-packing before I knew much about deer hunting. In those days I packed all over the eastern Sierras, fishing for golden trout and enjoying the solitude and peace of mind that true wilderness gives.

Making the transition from a general backpacker to a backpack deer hunter was relatively easy for me. I was familiar with the latest equipment, and had learned by trial and error what to bring and what to leave behind, how to pick a campsite, how to layer my clothing, and how important it was to stay warm and dry.

My first backpack deer hunts were made in southern California's coastal mountains, some of the steepest, brushiest and most rugged country I've ever traveled. After high school I began traveling to distant states to hunt mule deer. Being a starving college student, I couldn't afford horses or guides. The only way I could access the backcountry—where hunters were few and deer many—was on shank's mare. These early trips taught me how to care for meat in the field, how to bone a carcass and keep it clean and how much work it can be. But oh, how I loved it! Here was a way to get the best hunting for minimal money. And even today, the feeling of accomplishment following a successful backpack hunt remains unsurpassed.

GETTING AWAY FROM IT ALL

One fact I've learned over the years is that consistently successful public land mule deer hunters know they must get away from other hunters whenever possible. Those who pay the price in sweat equity have a much better chance of bagging a good buck than those who stick to the roads or their ATVs. On do-it-yourself hunts, I've tried escaping crowds two ways.

Every now and then, I'll leave my roadside camp shortly after midnight and climb high up timbered ridges, hoping to be in position at the crack of dawn. I'll hunt hard in the morning, take a nap midday, then hunt hard until dark, making my way back down

Solitude and good numbers of undisturbed deer—that's what makes all the hard work of backpack hunting worthwhile.

the mountain by flashlight.

But the best way is to backpack camp into the wilderness, bringing enough food and gear to stay a week or more. While backpacking is hard work (and getting harder every year as my bones grow older), it is still the least expensive way to give yourself a better-than-average chance at one of the West's best public land bucks.

Later in this book you'll read about other aspects of backpack hunting, notably physical conditioning, researching the hunt, meat care and dressing properly. But the next few pages are focused on the equipment you'll need to make backpack hunting a realistic option. When selecting backpack hunting gear, remember the phrase "performance without weight." You need gear that will get the job done without an extra ounce to make an already difficult job even tougher.

THE HUNTING PACK

Backpack hunters need a stout backpack with a large bag to carry their camp and gear into the woods, and pack the meat, cape and antlers back to the road. If you haven't looked at backpacks in five years, you'll be amazed at how they've evolved. Companies like Eureka!, Camp Trails, Badlands, Kelty, Lowe Alpine Systems and Dana Designs are producing the finest

large-capacity, lightweight packs ever made.

Your pack bag needs plenty of outside pockets for stuffing items like water bottles, first aid kit, maps, and the like. The frame must have a harness system designed for heavy loads, be adjustable so it can be fitted exactly to your body, and feature triple stitching that won't rip out when the going gets tough. You'll also need to get a rain cover for your pack—they cost about 20 bucks—to keep it dry.

It is very important to adjust your pack's harness system to fit you properly. This will determine how and where the weight and stress of your load rests on your body. Proper loading makes carrying lots of weight much easier than an unbalanced load. All quality packs come with adjustment instructions.

I also like to bring along a fanny or daypack, which I use as my daily hunting pack. That way I can move easier, quieter and with less weight through deer country than when carrying my haul-everything pack and bag. Fieldline, Crooked Horn Outfitters and White Buffalo Outdoors make excellent packs for this job. I store everything inside my packs in either a plastic trash bag (heavy-duty trash compactor bags are the best for this) or in zip-top bags, which keeps them both dry and dust-free.

Choosing equipment for a backpack hunt is as much a process of elimination as anything else. You want to take everything you need, and not a single ounce more.

The best place to find cutting-edge backpack equipment is in a specialty mountaineering or backpacking store. You should be able to find a tent, sleeping bag and pad that weigh less than 10 pounds. That's total.

GIMME SHELTER

You have to have adequate shelter when backpacking. Regardless of where or when you hunt, you can count on at least part of the trip involving rain, snow, high winds—or all three. In addition, you have to sleep comfortably and well to allow your body to recover from the rigors of wilderness hunting on foot. Yet camp can't weigh a ton. All together, my three-season tent, sleeping bag and pad weigh just nine pounds, and have kept me warm and dry in heavy rains, winds of over 75 miles per hour, deep snows and temperatures near zero degrees. A space blanket can serve as an emergency shelter and, together with parachute cord, can be rigged into a small lean-to for cooking, drying wet clothes and sitting up outside the tent at night.

There are two tent options. A standard two-man backpacking tent has enough room for one person plus some gear, while a three-man tent is about right for two average-sized guys and a little "stuff." Make sure your tent has a quality rain fly. Before the season, I lightly spray my fly down with a silicone, like Camp Dry, to give it added waterproofness. Your tent should also have long stakes—I buy aftermarket plastic stakes, because those that come with the tents are often too

flimsy for use in high winds and snow—and grommets that allow you to stake both the tent and the fly snugly down. You'll need some extra parachute cord for this. Quality three-season, three-man tents will weigh between four and six pounds.

The other option is a one-man bivvy sack. Bivvies are nothing more than a glorified sleeping bag cover with a little bit of head and body room provided by a minimal pole system. I like bivvy sacks for early-season hunting, when I'm not expecting horrible rains or snow. Their saving grace is their size and weight. They roll up into a small stuff sack, and weigh less than 1½ pounds.

Sleeping bags should feature synthetic—not down—insulation. Synthetics provide nearly as much warmth per pound but, unlike down, retain a high percentage of their insulating abilities when wet. Prima-Loft, Polartec, Polarguard, Micro-loft, Quallofil and Hollofil II are all good insulation materials of this type. You'll also need a light sleeping pad to get your body off the ground. The pad's size and thickness depends on how cold it will be. Therm-A-Rest makes an excellent line of self-inflating pads that weigh just ounces and are very comfortable.

LET'S EAT

While I eliminate ounces in my backpacking gear, the one area I won't scrimp on is food. Wilderness hunting is hard work, and your body needs plenty of calories to keep it going. On hunts of a week or more, I pack one freeze-dried dinner per person per day. Breakfast is built around instant oatmeal, while midday meals and snacks are centered around meat sticks, jerky and granola bars. I also pack some dried fruit and Carbo Fuel, a concentrated carbohydrate powder that, when mixed with water, helps boost your energy level during strenuous exercise. Tang is delicious and a great energy booster too. At times I've packed tubes of peanut butter, a roll or two of bagels, a brick of cheese and some hard candies. I always take a multivitamin tablet each day too.

My kitchen consists of a small backpack stove,

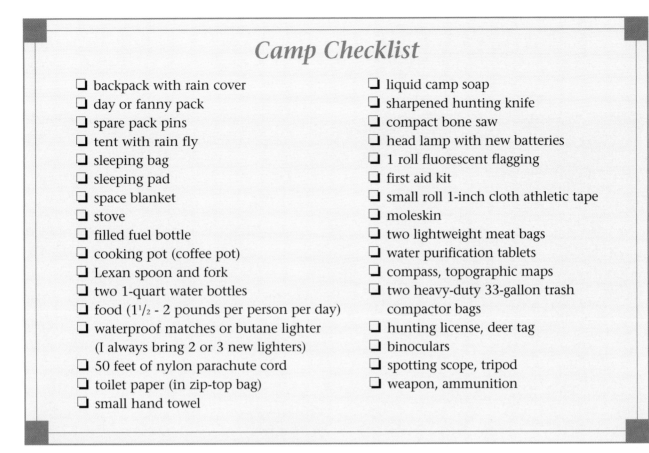

Camp Checklist

- ❏ backpack with rain cover
- ❏ day or fanny pack
- ❏ spare pack pins
- ❏ tent with rain fly
- ❏ sleeping bag
- ❏ sleeping pad
- ❏ space blanket
- ❏ stove
- ❏ filled fuel bottle
- ❏ cooking pot (coffee pot)
- ❏ Lexan spoon and fork
- ❏ two 1-quart water bottles
- ❏ food (1½ - 2 pounds per person per day)
- ❏ waterproof matches or butane lighter (I always bring 2 or 3 new lighters)
- ❏ 50 feet of nylon parachute cord
- ❏ toilet paper (in zip-top bag)
- ❏ small hand towel

- ❏ liquid camp soap
- ❏ sharpened hunting knife
- ❏ compact bone saw
- ❏ head lamp with new batteries
- ❏ 1 roll fluorescent flagging
- ❏ first aid kit
- ❏ small roll 1-inch cloth athletic tape
- ❏ moleskin
- ❏ two lightweight meat bags
- ❏ water purification tablets
- ❏ compass, topographic maps
- ❏ two heavy-duty 33-gallon trash compactor bags
- ❏ hunting license, deer tag
- ❏ binoculars
- ❏ spotting scope, tripod
- ❏ weapon, ammunition

You need lots of calories when backpacking, yet you can't carry a bunch of bulky food. I prefer foods with at least 100 calories/ounce of dried weight, and figure on about 1 to 2 pounds of food per person per day.

filled fuel bottle, small aluminum coffee pot for boiling water, a Lexan spoon and fork and two quart-sized water bottles, which I pack hunting each day. You can eat the freeze-dried dinners right from the pouch; I

cook the oatmeal in the coffee pot.

The secret is to bring foods that are high in their calorie content per ounce, yet also provide proper nutrition. I like foods that provide at least 100 calories per ounce of dried weight. Figure on packing 1½ to 2 pounds of food per person per day on a backpack hunt.

WHERE CAN I FIND THIS STUFF?

The best place to find cutting-edge tents, sleeping bags, backpacks and other state-of-the-art backpacking equipment, plus personnel knowledgeable in their use, is a specialty backpacking or mountaineering store. Some large mail-order hunting companies and a few large hunting stores carry some backpacking equipment, but they can't beat the specialty shops for this kind of equipment or expert help in selecting the right gear.

One word of caution: When you're shopping and see all the neat stuff for sale in a well-stocked backpacking store, remember one thing—you have to carry every ounce of it. Bring everything you need, but remember the cardinal rule of backpack hunting—less is definitely more.

DAYPACK ESSENTIALS

Western hunters need large-volume, well-designed daypacks, not the small fanny or teardrop packs treestand whitetail hunters commonly carry. Why? Because in addition to regular, everyday hunting stuff and depending on the time of year, on mule deer hunts you'll need to carry an assortment of bulky gear that includes: a rain suit; warm jacket, hat and gloves; lunch; water; and more. You'll likely be carrying your pack over many miles of broken country, and you'll use it whether you're leaving your tent camp at the crack of dawn or you've parked your rig and are heading up the mountain for a day. If your daypack is not comfortable to carry, you'll be miserable and less efficient than you would otherwise be.

THE PACK

A topnotch hunting daypack features an outer-shell material of either polar fleece or one of the new soft, quiet nylon fabrics like Stealth Cloth or Saddle Cloth that are whisper-quiet when going through brush. It will have large, adjustable shoulder straps to help evenly distribute weight. The waist belt and chest strap will be easily adjustable and will feature quick-detach buckles of high-impact plastic. Side pockets will be large enough for a water bottle or spotting scope, plus there will be smaller pockets for lesser items. Some top-quality daypacks feature a leather or reinforced bottom pad to guard against wear and tear. A waterproof liner inside the main compartment is useful. Companies like Fieldline, Crooked Horn Outfitters, Badlands and White Buffalo Outdoors make excellent daypacks, as do mail-order houses like Cabela's and Bass Pro Shops.

Some hunters like to carry packs that are a bit larger, including both internal and external frame models. That way they can carry all their day-hunt equipment (even enough for a day or spike-out), and then, if they get their deer, can bone it out and pack it back without having to make another trip. One classic pack design of this type is the Dwight Schuh Hunting Pack, designed by *Bowhunter* magazine editor Dwight Schuh. It features a medium-sized fleece upper bag and lower fleece fanny-type bag, both attached to a plastic Coleman Junior external frame.

Internal frame packs designed for western hunters that have lots more room, weigh little and are made from quiet outer shell materials are also made by Eureka! and Badlands. White Buffalo Outdoors of Morgan, Utah, makes the Mountain Master pack. This excellent pack features a roomy fanny pack design, but also includes a lightweight collapsible external frame. When you get your deer, you can quickly build the frame into the existing pack, and use it in conjunction with a game meat sack to pack your boned-out deer back to camp.

It's important to make sure your daypack's shoulder straps can be snugged firmly against your shoulders. For some reason many pack designers build their packs for oversized men with weightlifter chests or beer bellies. Unless the pack can be cinched tightly on your body, carrying heavy loads will be uncomfortable and unnecessarily fatiguing.

Here's a bonus use for your daypack. When glassing for long periods of time—for a serious mule deer hunter, this can be endless hours—try using your pack as a seat cushion. It will not only cushion that hard ground, but keep those small, sharp rocks, sticks and thorns from peppering your behind.

What to Carry

Telling a hunter what to carry in his pack is a lot like telling him which flavor of ice cream to eat. Some like chocolate, some vanilla. You will decide what to carry in your day-pack based on what you want to carry but also based on the time of year, the terrain you're hunting and whether or not you're hunting alone. Still, basic survival items always should go with you whenever you step into the woods. The rest can be added and subtracted depending on the time of year. My daypack first-aid items are minimal, but I always have more extensive items in base camp, just in case. A list of basic daypack items can be found in the sidebar on page 66.

Some items are also determined by the type of pack you carry. For example, I am a big believer in using a rest when shooting my rifle. Over the years I've found that I can shoot very well from the sitting position, especially when shooting on a rounded slope at a downhill angle—the situation I find myself in a lot when hunting mulies. When I hunt out of an external frame pack, I can sit down and use the top bar of the pack to create a very solid rest. When I hunt from a smaller daypack, I might carry a lightweight set of shooting sticks, like those from Stoney Point Products, which provide the same solid shooting platform.

One advantage to a medium-sized hunting pack featuring a solid external frame: It can double as a solid rifle rest. I've shot more big game this way than I can remember.

Practice shooting with your daypack on, in case a good buck suddenly appears and you don't have time to shed it before taking the shot.

I also like to organize my daypack stuff, using both quart- and half-gallon-sized heavy-duty zip-top bags. In one I might have my skinning knife, rubber butchering gloves and a small whetstone. Another might hold my fire starter materials, lighter and small first aid kit. One always holds a half roll of toilet paper. Because things are grouped according to their uses and I can see through the clear plastic bags, I can find everything quickly without dumping my pack completely out on the ground. The bags also protect my gear from rain and dust.

Your daypack and its contents are personal things. Over time you'll learn what you do and don't need. Be meticulous in choosing your pack, make sure it fits you correctly and fill it with those items that will help make you a more efficient deer hunter. You'll be glad you did.

Daypack Items

- ❏ hunting license, deer tag
- ❏ 1 or 2 quart-sized water bottles
- ❏ compass with mirror
- ❏ topographic maps
- ❏ butane lighter or waterproof matches
- ❏ fire starter material
- ❏ space blanket
- ❏ flashlight or head lamp—fresh batteries
- ❏ rangefinder, extra battery
- ❏ sharpened hunting knife, whetstone
- ❏ 50 feet of nylon parachute cord
- ❏ assorted Band-Aids
- ❏ small roll 1-inch cloth athletic tape
- ❏ moleskin
- ❏ Ibuprofen tablets
- ❏ personal medications
- ❏ spare eyeglasses
- ❏ lunch/snacks
- ❏ toilet paper in zip-top bag
- ❏ 1 roll fluorescent flagging
- ❏ 2 lightweight meat sacks

As dictated by season or conditions add:
- ❏ warm gloves
- ❏ stocking hat
- ❏ light vest or jacket
- ❏ packable Gore-Tex rain suit

BOWHUNTING EXTRAS

Your bowhunting daypack should always contain a spare release aid or finger tab and the proper-sized Allen wrenches for your bow and accessories, "just in case."

Smart muley bowhunters are constantly doping the wind. Fill a small puff bottle with unscented cornstarch or powdered carpenters chalk, or use API Outdoors' Windfloaters for quick, easy wind direction monitoring.

DRESS FOR SUCCESS

From the Canadian Rockies to the deserts of old Mexico, mule deer hunters experience everything from very hot and dry, to cold and rainy, to frigid sleet and snow. To remain comfortable and safe, and to hunt at peak efficiency, you must dress properly.

The key is to view your hunting clothing as a system, not as several different pieces that are each entities unto themselves. In this system all the parts must work together to provide a micro-climate for the body that keeps it warm but not hot, cool but not cold and offers protection against the elements. To be most effective, your garments must be designed for the conditions at hand.

Layering your clothing is the only way to dress for mule deer hunting these days. That way you can add or subtract layers as needed, staying comfortable and dry all day long. A wicking layer of synthetic underwear should always be your base layer.

THE IMPORTANCE OF LAYERING

Rather than wear one heavy jacket over a thin shirt, it is better to wear several thinner garments that can be removed and/or vented when you're too hot, then put back on or closed up when you're too cold. For example, hiking up a steep mountainside makes the body hot, so you need layers on top that can either be removed and carried, or zipped open or unbuttoned to allow body heat to escape. Once you're on top of the mountain, you can add layers as your body begins to recover from the exertion of the climb and starts to cool down.

First layers should be a wicking-type synthetic underwear of Thermax, Coolmax or another high-tech fabric that both insulates and wicks moisture vapor—sweat—off the body. Removing this moisture is the key to staying comfortable, one reason cotton long johns—which lose their insulative values when wet—are a no-no.

OUTERWEAR

Subsequent layers should be made of breathable materials that continue to permit moisture vapor to escape to the outside of the clothing system. Wool and synthetic materials like polarfleece will do this. Your outerwear must do two things—protect you from brush and rocks, as well as the elements, and remain quiet. That's one reason smart buck hunters never wear scratchy nylon or denim and instead select fleece, wool or synthetics with a soft hand.

Two breathable high-tech materials that also block 100 percent of

Scent-blocking garments featuring activated carbon are being worn by more and more mule deer hunters each year. Both stand hunters and spot-and-stalkers will find these garments highly useful in the ever-swirling winds of the West.

the wind and are laminated to many different outerwear shell fabrics are Gore-Tex and Windstopper. Gore-Tex is also 100 percent waterproof and can be found in superb lightweight, packable rain suits from companies like Whitewater Outdoors, Browning and 10X, among others, as well as pants, jackets, gloves, caps and hunting boots. Windstopper is designed for active hiking. I've found that wearing lightweight Windstopper shirts, gloves and caps allows me to wear several layers less than in the "old days," before this laminate became available. That translates into less weight and bulk and, as a result, a more efficient hunter.

SCENT-BLOCKING GARMENTS

Scent-blocking clothes aren't just for whitetail hunters. Mule deer have excellent noses, too. One whiff of human scent, and that's it—it's all over. For this reason, more and more mule deer hunters have begun incorporating scent-blocking garments into their clothing systems. This is especially true of those hunting around large agriculture fields, from ground blinds or treestands, and on day hunts.

Contemporary scent-blocking garments employ activated carbon (charcoal), which adsorbs (yes adsorbs, defined by Webster's as "to take up and hold") human scent and prevents these odors from reaching game. Both underwear—worn under your regular hunting outerwear, which ideally has been freshly laundered in no-scent laundry detergent—and outerwear are available. The latest outerwear garments feature an outer shell of quiet, soft synthetic cloth, making it ideal even for close range hunting, like bowhunting.

Scent-blocking garments for hunting were pioneered by Scent-Lok, and this is still an excellent product. W.L. Gore's Supprescent, which imbeds the activated carbon into the company's Windstopper membrane, is another great product. The end result is high performance outerwear that blocks both human scent and 100 percent of the wind, yet is highly breathable, thereby reducing the number of underlayers I need to wear. And you can wash Supprescent garments in your washing machine with no loss of effectiveness. Whitewater Outdoors, Browning, Redhead (Bass Pro Shops) and 10X all produce Supprescent garments suitable for all big game hunting.

What to Wear

UNDER LAYERS

Wear Capilene or Thermax long johns, and don't forget wicking socks. Thorlo, Whitewater Outdoors and Wigwam make good hiking and hunting socks.

OUTER LAYERS

During the early season, fleece pants and jackets are excellent. Later on, wool pants and shirts or Gore-Tex fleece pants and jackets are super. The new Gore Windstopper shirt from Whitewater Outdoors is lightweight, windproof and made from silent Stealth cloth; it helps eliminate additional layers. Add or subtract layers as conditions dictate.

FOOTWEAR

Bob-type soles offer excellent traction. Gore-Tex boots are waterproof and breathable. Choose insulation level based on the time of year and weather. Rubber-bottom, leather-upper pac boots are best for the cold and deep snow of very late seasons.

HEAD & HANDS

You will need a billed cap, stocking cap and gloves. During bow season, don't forget a head net or CarboMask face paint. Thin polypropylene glove liners are valuable.

RAINWEAR

With silent outer fabric, the new lightweight, packable Gore-Tex rain suits from Whitewater Outdoors, 10X and Browning are superb for active mule deer hunting.

Late-season hunters battling snow and bitter cold will find it hard to beat traditional wool outerwear.

FOOTWEAR

Western hunting boots must be rugged enough to offer ankle support and withstand the abuse of the toughest terrain, yet also breath and remain waterproof. Gore-Tex boots with an aggressive bob-type sole are the finest all-around all-season hunting boot of this type, offering breathability, waterproofness and toughness. Companies like Danner, Georgia Boot, Wolverine, Rocky Boots and Northlake build excellent boots. During early bow seasons some archers prefer lightweight canvas shoes or low cut boots.

In the dead of winter, pac-type boots are the way to go. Schnee's, Hodgman, LaCrosse, Rocky Boots and Sorel make excellent winter hunting boots.

HEAD & HANDS

The body loses more body heat from the head than any other place. Don't overlook protecting both the head and hands in cool weather. Carrying a stocking-type cap and pair of light gloves in the daypack will allow you to stay warm while glassing from high atop a windy ridge. In winter, of course, heavier hats and gloves are essential.

Choosing the Right Boots & Socks

Mule deer hunters need rugged, dependable and comfortable boots to successfully navigate the wilderness. However, not all boots are right for every hunting situation. In mountainous areas, the country is steep and jumbled. In the desert, it is relatively flat. Some areas are wet, some dry; some are hot, some cold. You need a boot designed for the specific conditions at hand.

"The human foot was really not designed to wear a shoe or boot," says Tom Casti, Hunting Footwear Product Specialist for W.L. Gore & Associates, makers of the Gore-Tex and Windstopper membranes. "Wearing the wrong boot during strenuous hunting activities can be both uncomfortable and damaging to the foot and entire lower body. Choosing the right boot—especially for a strenuous activity like hunting—will help prevent recurring foot problems and permit the outdoorsman to enjoy his or her sport at full speed."

The most important step in picking the right hunting boot is to choose a boot style with features designed for your specific activity, then get properly fitted. For all western hunting, including desert and flat-ground hunting, I've found that an aggressive sole is critical. The best is an airbob-type sole, which gives superb traction on all types of terrain. This is true even in snow, when pac-type boots are worn.

"Wearing an insulated boot for hunting in hot weather will cause the foot to sweat, and therefore, increase discomfort and potential foot problems," Casti says. "A boot with soft, smooth soles may be great for upland bird hunting, but poor for climbing western mountains. Boots with high uppers are great in the mountains, but may be too hot or confining in flatter country. Fortunately, hunters have a large choice of brands from which to choose; many feature a Gore-Tex bootie designed to make those boots waterproof and breathable, both important factors in performance and comfort."

You need sturdy, comfortable boots that have been broken in.

Wear a thin wicking sock first, followed by a thicker outer sock.

Casti recommends visiting a shoe or boot store with a wide boot selection and trained sales people to measure your feet with a Brannock device. "The Brannock device is the only way to get a precise foot measurement that includes foot length, width and arch height," Casti says. "People should realize that the proper boot size will vary by manufacturer, and even between different boot models from the same manufacturer. Also, your foot size will change over the years. A boot size that fit 10 years ago may not be the right size for you today. If you haven't recently had your foot measured with this device, you may be wearing the wrong size shoes and boots."

Also important is choosing the right sock system for hunting, and trying on your new boots with the same socks you'll be wearing afield. "W.L. Gore recommends wearing a thin wicking sock made of polypropylene under a well-made, padded outer sock made from synthetic materials, wool or a wool/synthetic blend," Casti says. "This will help cushion and protect the foot inside the boot, as well as wick perspiration away from the foot and out through the Gore-Tex bootie, keeping the feet dry. We don't recommend cotton socks because they will absorb moisture and can cause all sorts of problems like chilled, clammy feet and blisters."

For more information on proper boot fit and selection, contact W.L. Gore & Associates, 105 Vieve's Way, Elkton, MD, 21921, (800) 410-4673.

SHAPING UP

I made my first wilderness backpack hunt for mule deer in 1968 at age 16. It remains my favorite way to hunt all big game, and especially big muley bucks. Over the years I've learned two things. The mountains don't care that you're getting older, they're still steep and tough. And waiting until the week before opening day is too late to train your body for what lies ahead.

The most important thing in wilderness hunting is being fit enough to get the job done. That means improving your aerobic capacity. Aerobic literally means "with oxygen," which is the fuel that drives our bodies. Simply put, the more oxygen your body can process in a given amount of time, the more work it is able to do. To be able to hunt longer and harder, you have to train your body for the challenge.

Here's how to get ready for mountain hunting.

FIVE STEPS TO SUCCESS

1 **Have a medical examination.** If you haven't been exercising regularly, visit your doctor for a complete checkup. This is especially important if you're over 40 years old. Once given the okay, you're ready to start.

2 **Determine your "target heart rate" (THR).** To gain maximum benefits from an aerobic exercise program, you must maintain

A Basic Fitness Program

While each individual has his or her own needs and abilities, likes and dislikes, here is a basic jogging program that will markedly improve your aerobic capacity in 12 weeks. It is designed for both men and women 30 to 49 years of age who have not been exercising regularly, but who have been cleared by their physician to begin an exercise program. The time goals are designed to be met at the end, not the beginning, of the week. A walk is defined as covering a mile in more than 14:01 minutes; walk/jog 12:01-14:00 minutes per mile; and jog 9:00-12:00 minutes per mile.

To begin with, it is best if you run or jog on nonconsecutive days. On the days in between aerobic workouts, you can incorporate your calisthenics and/or weight training regimen. And while you never want to go too many days between workouts, taking a day off once a week will both help your body recover fully and actually enhance the training effect of your program.

Week	Activity	Distance (miles)	Time Goal (minutes)	Frequency/Week
1	walk	2.0	34	3
2	walk	2.5	42	3
3	walk	3.0	50	3
4	walk/jog	2.0	25	4
5	walk/jog	2.0	24	4
6	jog	2.0	22	4
7	jog	2.0	20	4
8	jog	2.5	26	4
9	jog	2.5	25	4
10	jog	3.0	31	4
11	jog	3.0	29	4
12	jog	3.0	27	4

a sufficiently high heart rate during exercise. Your THR is the maximum rate your heart should be beating during exercise. You determine your THR by first calculating your Predicted Maximum Heart Rate (PMHR). Here's the PMHR calculation: For a woman, subtract your age from 220 (for a 35-year-old woman, that's 185). For a man, subtract one-half of your age from 205. (For a 47-year-old like me, that's 181.5 beats per minute.) The THR is calculated by taking 80 percent of your PMHR (for me, that's 145 beats per minute; for the 35-year old woman, it's 148 beats per minute.) To achieve a training effect, you must exceed your THR for a minimum of 20 minutes, four times per week during exercise.

It is important to note that achieving the minimum training effect—20 minutes at or above your THR, four times per week—is just that, the minimum. The longer and harder you train, within reason, the better shape you'll be in. Just remember to start slowly and work your way up. In physical fitness, as in all good things in life, there are no shortcuts. Only a sustained effort over time will produce the desired results.

3 **Choose an aerobic exercise.** Aerobic exercises must get your heart pumping at your THR and also be an activity, or combination of activities, that interest you enough so you'll stick with it over time. Jogging, swimming, bicycling, walking, jumping rope

Weight down a pack and exercise on the biggest, steepest hill you can find near home, to get your legs ready for the climbing involved in a mule deer hunt.

and roller blading are good examples. The step aerobics classes so popular at local health clubs are an excellent way both to improve your overall aerobic capacity and to tone up your muscles. You can incorporate part of your training into your daily life too. Instead of riding the elevator or escalator, take the stairs. When walking to and from the office, walk briskly. Don't park as close to the store as possible, park in the back of the lot. Begin consciously thinking about ways to make your body work a little harder every day.

4 **Add strength and flexibility training.** Aerobic exercise isn't enough. You need to train your muscles and increase flexibility too. This means weight training or calisthenics, like push-ups, pull-ups, sit-ups and stretching. When using weights, concentrate on the main muscle groups—legs, back, shoulders, arms, chest and stomach. However, don't forget that the most important muscle in your body is your heart. It is best strengthened through aerobic exercise.

5 **Start now!** While it's never too late to begin, each day you wait to begin your conditioning program is one day closer to opening day. Starting a regular training program three months prior to a wilderness hunt is enough time to measurably increase your ability to navigate the mountains. Six months is better.

Calories Burned from Physical Activity

Activity	Calories/hour	Time to Burn 250 Calories
Walking (4.5 mph)	400	45 minutes
Roller skating, blading (moderate)	354	45 minutes
Swimming (crawl, 45 yards/min.)	530	30 minutes
Handball, Racquetball	600	25 minutes
Tennis (moderate)	425	35 minutes
Tennis (vigorous)	600	25 minutes
Jogging (5.5 mph)	650	22 minutes
Biking (13 mph)	850	18 minutes

Comparing Exercise Types

Activity	Aerobic Capacity	Strength
Weight training only	No change, possible decrease	Over 30% increase
Aerobic training only	15–25% increase	0–12% increase
Circuit weight training (30 sec. of rest between exercises)	5% increase	18% increase
Supercircuit training (jog in place, skip rope, use stair-step or cross-country ski machine for 30 sec. between exercises)	12% increase	23% increase

(Statistics for all three sidebars taken from *The Aerobics Program For Total Well-Being,* by Dr. Kenneth Cooper, MD., M.P.H., M. Evans & Co., New York, NY, 1982.)

SPECIFICITY TRAINING

In the beginning you'll want to concentrate on general fitness. However, as hunting season draws near, it's time to add to your program what exercise physiologists call "specificity training"—exercises designed to improve the performance of a specific task. For example, because wilderness hunters spend lots of time hiking and climbing while carrying a loaded pack, you should include exercises that simulate these activities in your basic fitness program.

In early summer I go for long walks, starting out for an hour or so at a good pace wearing a 20-pound daypack. As opening day gets closer, I start carrying my backpack with increasingly heavy loads, working up to about 80 pounds. I don't carry that every day, but I try to get my muscles used to that load. It's also very important not to limit yourself to training just on flat ground; you should also climb. Stadium steps, hills and the stair machine at the gym all factor into this program.

HOW DO I GET STARTED?

Receiving professional advice and guidance to achieve a fitness goal today is as easy as joining a local health club, YMCA or signing up for a class at the local college or other accredited institution specializing in physical fitness. Most employ trained professionals who can help you design an exercise program to meet your specific goals, as well as help keep you motivated.

Maintaining a year-round fitness program makes getting in shape for hunting season so much easier, especially as you get older. Sure, there are days I don't want to drag myself to the gym or go out for a run. When that happens, I dream about that big buck I'm going to find this fall, living in some out-of-the-way back country hellhole. Unless I stick with the program, getting my body to where he lives will be out of the question.

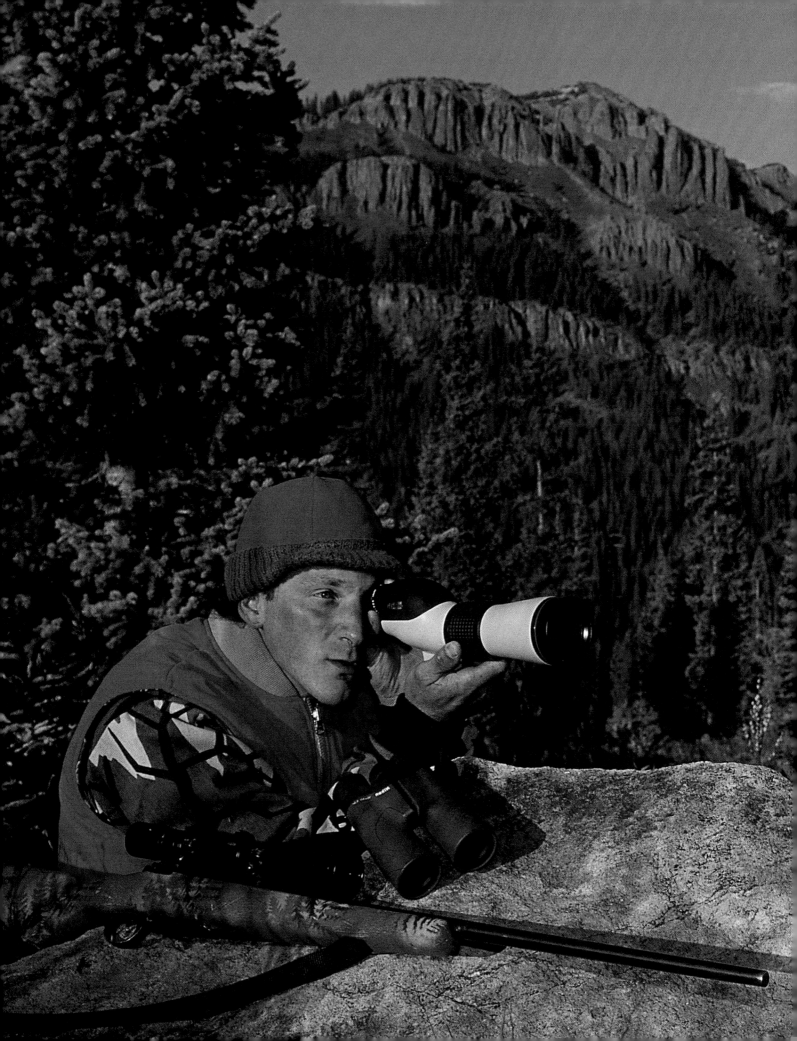

HOW TO HUNT MULE DEER

Some people like plain vanilla ice cream. They're the folks who like consistency and dependability in their everyday lives. No big surprises, no sudden changes in plans. For them, doing things the same way, day in and day out, is comforting.

I'm not like that. I do like vanilla, but I also like chocolate. And strawberry. And rocky road. I like the opportunity to do it a little differently from time to time, experience new things, test myself against fresh challenges. Maybe that's why I love mule deer hunting so much.

Mule deer hunters can be successful utilizing the entire bag of tricks. Spot-and-stalk hunting is the preferred method during most seasons, under the widest range of conditions. Top buck hunters have the equipment and skills to glass 'em up from August through December, from the high peaks to the desert.

But the best muley hunters I know attack the challenge from other angles too. Some have developed great skills as trackers and are able to read sign and follow a buck all day long until, finally, there he is, bedded just over there, without a care in the world. Every now and again, drives work well, with bucks squirting out of the bottoms of deep canyons and brushy draws into the waiting arms of the blockers. There are those who depend on days and days of scouting, then use what they find to help them set a treestand or build a ground blind over an isolated buck magnet, like a small spring seep. During the rut, adding a touch of calling and rattling just might tip the odds in your favor.

Then there are the different seasons. While I love my pet deer rifle, I love my bow just as much. My muzzleloaders are good friends too, as are my single-shot specialty pistols. Mule deer hunting offers me a chance to use them all each fall, during optimum season and conditions for success on better-than-average bucks.

The versatile mule deer hunter has the best chance of consistently tying his tag to a good buck. Does that sound like the kind of hunter you want to be? Then read on, and learn ...

SPOT-&-STALK SECRETS

As the old saying goes, there is more than one way to skin a cat. Mule deer hunting is no different. There are several proven techniques for consistently taking mulies. Some of them—notably tracking, driving and setting a stand—are detailed elsewhere in this chapter. But if I had to choose just one way to hunt mule deer, regardless of the season or the weapon I was carrying, it would be spot-and-stalk hunting.

Spot-and-stalk hunting is not still-hunting, whereby the hunter continually slips through relatively small patches of cover in search for game he's not sure is there. The still-hunter might be confident that he's in good deer country, but he is not actively stalking a particular animal. Stalking, on the other hand, does not begin until you locate—by spotting—the animal you want to hunt. It is at that time, and not before, when you begin sneaking in, trying for your shot.

Spot-and-stalk hunting is the classic way to hunt virtually all western big game. The vast expanses of the West, which enable you to see for miles and miles, makes this the most practical and efficient way to locate the maximum amount of game in the least amount of time. Here are the key advantages of the spot-and-stalk method.

The vast, wide-open spaces of the West were made for the spot-and-stalk hunter. In most cases, skilled spotters will find the most—and the biggest—bucks regardless of the time of year, local hunting pressure and the weather.

Large numbers of animals. No other hunting method allows you to look at as many deer in the least amount of time as does spotting from a good vantage point. When you spot deer from a long distance, you can do so without them having any idea you're around. That lets you watch them without fear of spooking them, which of course would send them either fleeing at top speed, or turning into "stealth deer," the kind that become so sneaky and, yes, even nocturnal, that your chances of getting a crack at them become minuscule.

Huntable deer. Just because you see lots of deer does not mean that you see lots of deer that are "huntable," that is, deer that are undisturbed and unaware of your presence. These deer will act like a deer normally would act, allowing you the opportunity to make your move. Also, by spotting them at long distance—if the deer are in a bad position for you to move in for a high-percentage shot—you can wait them out. When you see them first, you're in the driver's seat.

Pollution-free hunting. The older a muley buck gets, the smaller his home range becomes and the better he knows it. If you go tromping around his core area, you'll leave your scent lingering about, and he might hear, see or smell you. When that happens, you can be sure that he will become extremely difficult, if not impossible, to kill. That's evident after opening day of rifle season in areas with lots of hunter pressure. The deer—and especially the mature bucks—seem to vanish. They know something's up, and want no part of it. The better plan is to hunt from the fringes of good deer country, moving in only when the time is right to get a shot.

Selection. Whether you're on stand, or the blocker on a drive or simply still-hunting along, you are in a take-what-you-can-get situation. You have no idea what kind of bucks will come by and offer a shot. Conversely, by spending lots of time spotting, you can be very choosy (if you wish) about the deer you will try to tie your tag on.

Spot-and-stalk hunters should climb to a good vantage point, get comfortable, and let their eyes do the walking as they search for their dreams.

Efficiency. I'm not necessarily a lazy guy, but I don't like to waste time. Rather than spend all my time walking, I learned long ago that the most efficient way to hunt mulies was to climb to a high vantage point on the fringe of good buck country, plop down and let my eyes do the walking. Think about it. Even in great

deer country, only a small portion of the area actually holds deer. How can you best cover that country—by hiking randomly in the hopes you'll kick up a good buck, or sitting down and glassing them up?

PRIME-TIME BUCKS

One time I was sitting in a wall tent reading an outdoor magazine. The article was about hunting mulies, and it told about how tough it was to find a good buck. I must have had a very perplexed look on my face, because an old-timer came in and sat down beside me and offered me some advice. Back then I thought he was just "out of it." But today I know that he was right on the money. He said simply, "Son, the key to finding a good buck is to sit on your ass and glass, and don't be afraid of the dark."

Like a young bird dog, I was eager and full of get up and go. Instead of listening to him, I spent the next two seasons trying to see how many miles I could hike over that western Colorado mountain. I'd see deer, to be sure, and each year I shot a decent buck. But the old fellow always shot the biggest buck in camp. Finally, in the third year, I got up enough courage to

One big advantage to the spot-and-stalk method is that you will generally see deer before they see you. And when hunting smart old bucks—that can vanish like smoke on the wind at the first hint of danger—the importance of seeing them first cannot be overemphasized.

Mule Deer—Western Challenge

Once you've spotted a buck you want to stalk, take your time before charging off after him. Study the terrain, the wind, find any other deer in the area, and make a plan that will let you sneak within shooting range without the deer seeing, hearing or smelling you.

ask him how he did it. "Remember what I told you before?" he asked. When I shook my head he kindly invited me to hunt with him.

His method was simple. Every morning we left camp two hours before first light and slowly climbed to the top of a tall butte. We made ourselves comfortable, and when we could just begin to see, we began glassing. We stayed there all day, moving positions occasionally to provide different angles, and didn't leave our station until it was too dark to glass any more. We made it back to camp by flashlight.

After two days I was getting pretty bored. We'd seen some deer, sure, but nothing I didn't feel I could see by the usual method. Finally, on the third morning we spotted a dandy 4x4 slinking along a wash. We scrambled down off the butte, headed him off and the old-timer let me have first shot. It was my best buck up to that point and I was tickled. He even had the courtesy not to rub it in.

That's when the light bulb went on. The key to spotting both the maximum number of deer, and the biggest bucks, was not to be afraid to walk in the dark to and from a good glassing station. And once there, you had to keep diligently glassing.

Pretty simple, isn't it? And yet I meet hunters every year who are afraid of the boogeyman, or are scared they'll get lost in the dark, and so they are never on station in time. When spotting bucks, I'd trade all the rest of the day for the first and last hours of available light. That's when the most, and biggest, bucks are usually seen.

PLANNING THE STALK

Once you've spotted a buck you want, it's time to plan the stalk. How you go about stalking the deer is dependent on two things—the weapon you're hunting with and what the deer is doing.

Bowhunting. Bowhunters must be much more meticulous in their decisions than firearms hunters. After all, if you spook the buck you want with your bow, its "game over." Spook it while carrying a .270 and the rifle becomes your eraser, wiping out your mistake with its long-range killing power.

For that reason, when I bowhunt I much prefer to spot a buck in the morning, watch him go lay down, and try to stalk him in his bed. There are exceptions, of course. I've stalked to a good patch of cover in front of placidly feeding bucks and let them feed right

The first step to stalking a muley successfully is planning your approach carefully.

to me and my ready arrow. This is best done in broken country, where the natural folds in the land provide natural cover for you. Also, when bowhunting I find it much easier to stalk deer from above. Stalking from below is really hard to do. The bottom line is that you have to evaluate each situation as it comes, then make a "go" or "no go" decision based upon what's happening at that moment.

Rifle hunting. I follow the same basic game plan when planning a stalk with a rifle or muzzleloader as I do when bowhunting. That is, I want to get within comfortable shooting range of an undisturbed deer.

The long-range capabilities of these weapons makes that a much easier proposition, of course. My basic step-by-step program when planning a stalk goes something like this:

Assess the situation. Take in the whole world at that moment. Are there lots of deer, making the approach to the target deer problematic? How do I keep the sun at my back and wind in my face? What terrain features—draws, creekbottoms, timber stringers and brush—can I use for cover?

Where are the other deer? Never become so fixated on your target buck that you forget about any other deer that are with him. As often as not, these are the animals that will blow the stalk for you. Pinpoint their location before you leave, and be constantly on the lookout for them as you make your approach.

Lay of the land. If you stalk deer over long distances long enough, you'll soon find out that once you've made your stalk and gotten to within what you think is a close proximity to your deer, the country looks a whole lot different from where you're standing than it did from where you first spotted the animal. To eliminate this problem, Dwight Schuh, editor of *Bowhunter* magazine, showed me a trick one time that really helps. Dwight carries a small notebook and pen with him and draws a crude map before he begins his stalk. On it he marks his target deer, the position of other animals, plus prominent landmarks like big trees, gullies and large rocks. "In the excitement of the stalk, your memory is really unreliable," Dwight told me. "The map helps you remember things as they actually are, and it will really help you, especially when you get to the general area of the deer and you can't see him. You know he's still there, but your mind plays tricks on you, and unless you have faith in your skill and your map, you'll end up blowing the stalk." He's right. A compass is invaluable in this regard too.

Patience. By nature I'm an aggressive mule deer hunter. Once I spot the deer I want, my gut reaction is to rush over there and shoot him, right now! But I've learned that it is very important to stay under control and be patient, making your move only when the time is right. For example, when I see a buck go lie down, rather than rush over to try to shoot him, I wait 45 minutes to an hour and watch him. Often

Scrolling

Scrolling is a technique I use while hunting all types of game—but especially big mule deer. It's a good way to move about the country, looking for a buck to stalk. (And if you're rifle hunting, it's a good way to find a buck to shoot.)

Many hunters make the mistake of skylining themselves to the country they are hunting. If you learn to scroll, you'll prevent skylining and see more deer before they see you.

I call it scrolling because you "scroll" country as if you were rolling out an ancient scroll as you read it. Instead of just stumbling up and looking over a ridge to see what's on the other side, sneak up to that ridgeline and peek over, inch by inch, using the ridgeline as a scrolling line or ruler to slowly reveal the country you want to look at (see photo at right). Then move up a few inches more on that ridgeline, ever so slightly, and uncover a small but new amount of the country beyond. Each time you stop, thoroughly glass back and forth on the small sliver of landscape you have scrolled up. Once you've glassed that piece, move up a tad more and repeat.

You can scroll from your belly or your knees, or on your feet. I prefer to do it on my belly or knees, to lower my profile; plus, it's easier than crouching over all the time. If you choose to stay on your feet, make sure you have a backdrop of some sort to prevent skylining. And remember—we all tend to move too fast while we're on our feet, so be sure to inch along.

One of the big keys to scrolling is to break the landscape into narrow corridors 100 to 200 yards wide. Glass each corridor thoroughly, then move up a bit and break the next sliver into corridors. Once you expose an entire piece of country, back off, out of sight (the same way you came in), and move down the ridge a bit (approximately 200 yards) and scroll again. Make sure you look at the previous piece of landscape as well, because you'll now be looking at it from a different angle and viewing some hiding spots that weren't visible from your previous location.

By scrolling small portions of country at a time, you'll soon begin to spot mule deer long before they have a chance to spot you. This gives

Systematically "scrolling" the countryside while remaining off the skyline is a superb way to glass for mule deer bucks.

you the opportunity to back off and get into position for a better look, prepare for a shot or plan a stalk.

Now, I know this method sounds pretty tedious, but getting into the domain of a big buck mule deer—especially out in the wide open—is tough to do unnoticed. You'll never get to stalk him, let alone get a good shot, if he sees you first. Scrolling is my time-tested method for locating the bucks before they spot me.

—Jim Van Norman

Most stalks are blown because the hunter gets impatient and moves too fast. Take your time, be quiet as a church mouse, and constantly check the wind as you move into position.

bucks bed for an hour or so, then get up and move a short distance before bedding again. Usually when they do this they're bedded for hours, making stalking much easier. Waiting a bit also permits me to carefully scrutinize the country, look for other deer and define my stalking route. I call my method "controlled aggression."

GETTING THE SHOT

The technique is not called "spot-and-spook." The whole idea behind spot-and-stalk hunting is to spot an animal you want, then move in undetected for the shot. To that end, there are some things you need to do as you get close.

Most important is relocating the buck, especially if he's bedded in or near thick cover, or if you had to move behind some terrain features as you made your approach. This is the make-or-break point

in most stalks, regardless of your weapon. The key is to relocate the animal without being detected.

Meticulously use your binoculars to find him again. This is true even when bowhunting and the distance between you and the deer is relatively short. You're not necessarily looking for the whole deer, but just a piece of him—an antler tine, glossy black nose, an eye, a flicking ear or a horizontal backline in a vertical sea of lodgepole trunks. Sometimes a twitching tail will give him away. I've relocated more than one buck by first spotting one of the smaller satellite bucks I'd seen him with earlier. If they're still there, I know he is too, so I keep looking. Hard.

Be patient. Just because you don't see him right off the bat doesn't mean he's not there. Sure, he might have gotten up and fed off a ways, but unless he's panicked, he'll be close. My rule of thumb when stalking any animal is simply this—if I have not seen him run off with my own eyes, he's still there. So I keep looking.

Don't unnecessarily hurry. This point cannot be overemphasized. As sure as the sun rises in the east, you'll ruin more stalks by moving too fast, by becoming impatient, by letting your adrenaline overcome common sense, than you can shake a stick at. By the same token, unless you're stalking a quick-moving deer, you'll rarely improve your chances by hurrying.

Here's an extra tip: If you don't want him to hear you during your approach, first take off your boots, slip on a pair of thick wool socks, then finish the stalk. You'll be amazed at how quietly you can move.

Mule deer like to bed with their eyes facing open country and the wind at their backs, making it very difficult to sneak in on them. Watching a deer's head—the position of his ears will tell you everything you need to know—will tell you when it's safe to move closer.

HAND SIGNALS

Stalking a buck with a partner is extremely helpful. No, not if your buddy is trudging along behind you, making extra noise. Instead, one hunter moves in for the shot while the other remains on the spotting station, closely watching the buck and giving his partner hand signals.

You need a simple set of hand signals that tell the stalker he's getting close, the direction of the deer relative to the stalker's position, what the deer is doing (bedded, feeding, walking) and "everything's okay, keep going." You also need a signal that tells the stalker that the deer has run off, and the stalk's over. The key? Discuss and agree on the signals and their respective meanings before the hunt; you both need to be of the same understanding!

STAY FLEXIBLE

The best spot-and-stalk hunters are flexible in their approach. They know that conditions in the field change constantly, and they are able to "go with the flow" to be consistently successful. They know there's a time for patience and a time to move quickly; and a time to shoot and hold back. They know how and when to "push the envelope," staying aggressive, while not moving too boldly.

They also know that when the chips are down, the best way to find a good mule deer buck is by using the spot-and-stalk method. It's the foundation for all of their other mule deer hunting techniques. Once you see what the system can do, it will be the same for you too.

Spot-and-stalk hunting is the backbone of mule deer bowhunters. Stay flexible and move slowly and quietly; those are the keys to a successful stalk.

How to Hunt Mule Deer

HUNTING THE HIGH COUNTRY

*T*here are two prime time periods to hunt mule deer in the mountain country of the West—early and late.

The early season, depending on the state, generally runs from August through mid-September. It is characterized by long, sunny days punctuated with thunderstorms. The temperatures are relatively warm, and the high alpine bowls are as beautiful as they get, filled with lush green grasses highlighted by a kaleidoscope of multi-hued wildflowers.

The general rifle and late seasons are the other two general periods to hunt mule deer. The general rifle season usually takes place in October, after the bucks shed their velvet and before they begin to rut. The bucks are loners then, or matched up in pairs or small groups, and are tough to locate, especially if you're looking for the older patriarchs. The weather is mixed,

Hunting the high country in early season, any bucks you find will likely still be in velvet.

86

bringing both hot and cold days, dry and wet days, and if you're lucky, a little snow.

I define the late season as early November until the season closes—the antithesis of the early season. Temperatures plummet, the days shorten, and snows begin to fall. Icy winds blow off the polar caps, chilling you to the bone. But if you hit it right, the deer begin to rut, moving around a lot, and are relatively easy to spot.

The early season defines high-country mule deer hunting for me, though. In many cases, only archery or muzzleloader hunting is permitted, which tends to thin out the crowds. In fact, you'll find that most early-season hunters these days are chasing elk, not mulies. In August and early September, the deer are still in velvet, living their lives in the alpine bowls as they gorge on the high-quality food necessary to develop their antlers and stock up their body fat reserves for the coming winter. The deer are found feeding early and late in the day in these bowls, often bedding on their edges in the late morning, moving into the deep shade of the dark timber when it gets too hot. There they nap the day away, heading back out to feed in late afternoon.

Mule deer bucks can still be found in the high

In the mountains, high-country hellholes are perhaps the best places of all to find trophy-class muley bucks consistently.

country after the rifle seasons open in October too. However, once they lose the velvet off their antlers and human pressure picks up a little bit, they tend to drop into the dark timber or thick brushy canyons and draws, emerging only on the very cusp of daylight. (When it comes to becoming nocturnal, big whitetail bucks have nothing on mature mule deer that are

The first significant snow of the year in the high country will definitely get the bucks moving. When this occurs, it's time to drop everything and head for the hills!

How to Hunt Mule Deer

During the early season, bachelor groups of bucks can be found in high mountain meadow "pockets," gorging themselves on lush feed and enjoying cooling breezes.

THE POCKET PRINCIPLE

Early-season bucks gather in small bachelor herds of between three deer and a dozen or more. Usually these bachelor groups are comprised of deer of the same age, or of deer within a year or two of each other. Yearling bucks rarely are found with the bachelor groups, instead living with small herds of does and fawns.

It was a bright, sunny day in late August over 20 years ago in Nevada's Ruby Mountains that really hooked me on early-season bowhunting for mule deer. At this time of year, the deer have an almost reddish coat that literally glows in the bright sunlight. I glassed a giant bowl at the top of the peaks that must have been two miles across. In that bowl I counted 87 bucks scattered about in groups of between 3 and 15, all placidly feeding and enjoying the sunshine. The problem was, there were just too dang many deer! Every time I tried to make a stalk, there seemed to be another bunch of bucks in the way. I hunted for a week and never shot an arrow.

That's the exception—an experience I've never duplicated. More common is backpacking into the high country, setting up camp, and heading out in search of mule deer "pockets." When you get into a

pressured.) Here they spend the rest of the early and mid-season period, rarely leaving the sanctuary of this heavy cover. They can be very, very difficult to hunt at this time, especially for traveling hunters who do not know the terrain. The deer won't leave this thick cover until the late season, when either the rut, or deep snows—or both—force them out into the valleys below.

new piece of country, by using your topographic maps, then glassing the terrain, you'll see several areas that just look "deery." But you'll soon find that the majority of these places don't hold any deer. You cover some ground, and carefully glass many such areas before locating a bachelor herd of bucks. These small "pockets" define high country mule deer hunting in the early season.

I call it the "Pocket Principle." It says that 95 percent of good mule deer country holds no deer. All the deer are found in isolated pockets, where they live all summer.

A pocket can be one alpine bowl and a single patch of timber for cover and security. (In the flat lands of the plains it might be a single draw or gully in an area streaked with them.) More likely it is two or three adjacent bowls connected by saddles or strips of dark timber. The deer like to move between these bowls on a semi-regular basis, something I believe they do to keep from overbrowsing a specific bowl.

One year my friend Dwight Schuh and I backpacked into the rugged Sangre de Cristo Mountains of Colorado in search of some bigger-than-average mulies. We covered 10 to 15 miles a day for nearly two weeks. In that time, we found four pockets of mule deer bucks. After a time, we could almost predict where they'd be every morning and every afternoon. Some days, one bunch would be in alpine bowl "A," feeding happily along. The next day, that same bunch would move through a saddle to bowl "B." The third day, they might be in bowl "C." The fourth day, they were back in bowl "A." They lived in an area of about two square miles. Meanwhile, we hunted an area around them of about 10 square miles and never found another bunch of bucks.

FINDING THE DEER

Using topographic maps, you can pinpoint potential mule deer pockets before you ever get into the

Topographic maps are an essential tool of the mule deer hunter. They permit you to pre-plan a hunt by finding likely looking mule deer pockets before you ever set foot in the mountains.

country. Look for "fingers" along the edges of timber, set up against the highest peaks and adjacent to bowls. I look for streams too, although often the deer drink only from small seeps not found on any map. The north- and east- facing slopes usually get the most moisture during the year, and therefore, have the best food, so that's where I always start my search.

Once in the country, I climb to a high vantage point before first light and glass the pockets I located on my maps. If I see deer, great. If not, I glass other areas that just visually look good. By mid-morning, if I don't see anything exciting, I start covering ground, hiking and looking for standard deer sign like tracks, beds and so forth.

When moving, take care to stay in the shade, and keep the wind in your face at all times. The last thing you want is for your scent to spook unseen deer that may be bedded in the timber. I make a big circle from camp, glassing again from a high vantage point from late afternoon until it's too dark to see, hiking back to camp with the aid of a flashlight.

If I don't see any deer in a couple of days, I pack up camp and move five miles or more to another area my maps tell me has all the necessary ingredients, and I start the process all over again. Sooner or later I'll find the deer. When I do, it's time to begin hunting them in earnest.

THE RIGHT EQUIPMENT IS CRITICAL

When backpacking, you must have everything you need, and not an ounce more. For that reason, I eat only freeze-dried food right from the pouch, so I don't have to pack pots and pans. I drink powdered milk and Tang from my one-quart plastic bottle. I have one set of clothes, plus a rain suit, coat, stocking cap and spare socks. A lightweight sleeping bag, pad and small tent round it out. When there are two or three hunters, luxury items like a little solid food, can be added and divided among everyone.

Optics are where I don't scrimp on weight. You have to locate deer before you can hunt them, and there's no better way than with top-quality, powerful optics. I'm a firm believer in using tripod-mounted binoculars of between 15X and 20X for this kind of hunting. My 15x60 Zeiss glasses have found more deer in the high country that I would never have seen with lesser glasses. If I'm feeling spunky, I'll pack a small spotting scope, but usually my big binoculars are enough. I also carry a pair of compact 7X glasses for use when stalking.

HUNTING THE HIGH COUNTRY

Generally speaking, this is a spot-and-stalk game.

Maps are essential to navigating the backcountry. I write on my maps, noting deer magnets like seeps, water holes, a concentration of beds, preferred food sources and so on, so I can easily find these hot spots again and again.

You locate deer, watch them go lay down for the day, then try and stalk them in their beds. However, there are variations on this theme worth considering.

Mini drives between two hunters sometimes work. By patterning the deer, you can make an educated guess as to the trail they're likely to take out of a bowl when spooked. Station one shooter up on the trail and have the other try to herd the animals onto that trail. You have to drive "softly"; that is, just let the deer see you from afar, so that they'll move at a walk, not a panicked run.

"Sneak-and-Peek" Hunting

One of the simplest and most effective ways to hunt early-season mulies in the high country is what I call "sneak-and-peek" hunting. Here's how it works.

In high country hunting, it is almost always best to hike to a high vantage point in the dark, where you can set up and glass large expanses of country for deer from a hidden location. Often, though, you won't see what you want and will

Sneaking along ridgetops, then peeking over the edge and glassing for bedded bucks (remember, they love shade) is a great way to score during midday hours.

have to move. When moving, you must be careful not to skyline yourself and risk being spotted by unseen deer, who might pick you out from a mile or more away.

The secret is to traverse a high finger ridge that ideally borders some lush feeding meadows. At the upper edge of these meadows you'll often find large rock outcroppings or small patches of timber—ideal bedding areas. I move along the back side of the ridge for a ways, then carefully sneak to the top by crawling; I slowly peek over the edge and look for deer. I'll glass distant areas, but I regularly find the deer directly below me, oftentimes in bow range. If I don't see any deer, I drop back down below the ridgeline, move a ways, and repeat.

Sneak-and-peek hunting is a great way to hunt during midday, when bucks can often be found bedded under rimrocks. It also works well in lowland areas by sneaking along, then peeking over the edges of deep ravines and coulees. The key is keeping the wind right, and then peeking slowly over the edges, exposing as little of yourself as possible. Wearing either a face mask or camo face paint that takes the shine off your face is a good idea too. (The "Scrolling" sidebar, on page 83 in this chapter, provides important details related to sneak-and-peek hunting.)

Sometimes, placing a treestand along the edge of the dark timber or building a ground blind in the right spot is a good way to do business. I prefer stalking deer, simply because it's more flexible, and I'm able to adjust by the minute as the deer dictate. But there are times when a stand is a deadly technique.

Whatever you decide, keep in mind that it's always best to hunt unobtrusively. By not making any rash moves, like carelessly stinking up the area with your scent, and staying out of sight, you can hunt the same bachelor bunch of deer for a week or more without disturbing them.

High country mule deer hunting isn't for everyone. Admittedly, you need to be in pretty good physical condition to take on the rugged peaks for a week or more at a time. And I don't like heading into the back country for any less than a week. Every time I do, about the time I'm finally into the deer it's time to go home.

But the high alpine meadows in late August and early September are worth the price. And when you finally find that bachelor herd of a half-dozen mature bucks, with no other hunters in sight and a week ahead of you, you'll believe it was worth it too.

Pieces & Parts, Parts & Pieces
By Jim Van Norman

When looking for mule deer—whether you're in the high country, out on the prairie or anywhere in between—focus on *images*. This technique, which I call "pieces & parts," will make you a cut above the average mule deer hunter when it comes to spotting bucks.

Since mule deer—especially the bigger bucks—hide themselves so well, it is important to scan for very small parts, pieces or "images" rather than the whole deer. It is not extremely important to see those parts or pieces crystal-clear; you simply need to have a few images

engraved on your mind so that when your eyes scan over one, your brain stops all progress and returns your binoculars or spotting scope to that image.

There are actually 15 images consisting of five basic elements, with variations of each, and three geometric shapes in this concept. Don't panic! It's really quite simple, if you think of the five basic body-part images you're looking for.

I use the acronym "FERAL" to remember these basic body-part images that make up the 15 pieces and parts: F for Faces, E for Ears, R for Rumps, A for Antlers and L for Legs.

Faces—A mule deer's white face is often the first thing you'll see on a hiding buck. Other body parts might be camouflaged, but a stark white patch among the cover should be a tip for you to take another look. Then, as with the other images in this concept, slowly scan for the other parts attached to this part. For example: Attached to this stark-white patch is a round black nose, black chin stripe, white throat patch, dark forehead patch, the base of an antler, eyeball and so on.

Face Images to Look For:

Triangle of Dark Forehead Patch, Eyes and Black Nose

White Face and Muzzle

Side View of the Face

Ears—Keep ears at the top of your list when looking for hidden mule deer. An ear's "candle-flame" shape should immediately draw your attention. There are components within the shape, if another mule deer part isn't readily spotted, that I use to confirm the ear of a deer. Look for a gray outline and an inner lining of white. There is also a gray flap near the base of an ear. Plus, there may be a gray or black outline on the bottom of a mule deer's ear.

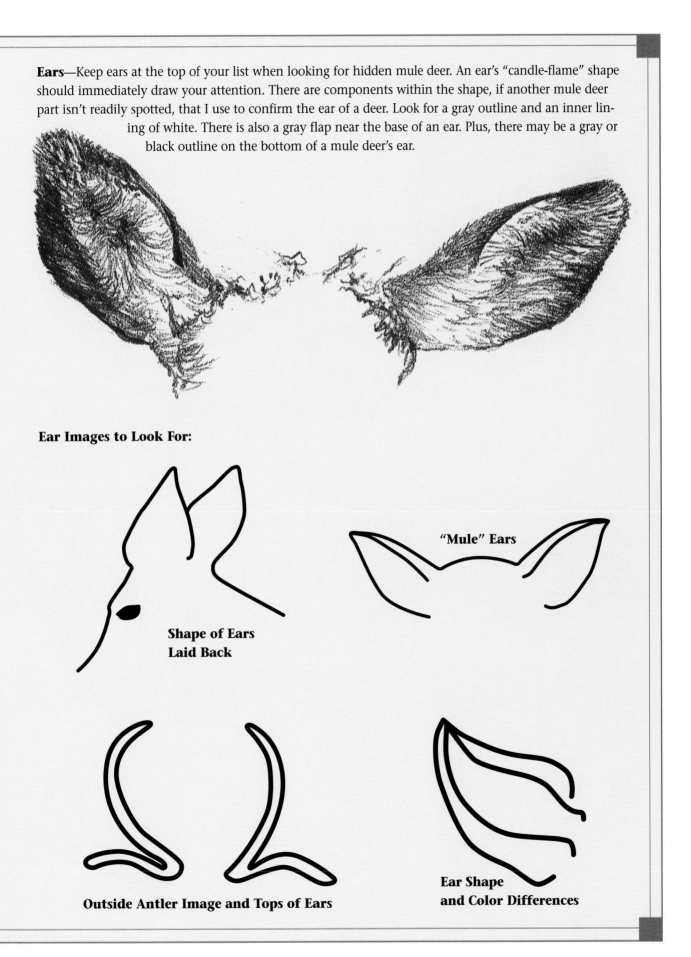

Ear Images to Look For:

**Shape of Ears
Laid Back**

"Mule" Ears

Outside Antler Image and Tops of Ears

**Ear Shape
and Color Differences**

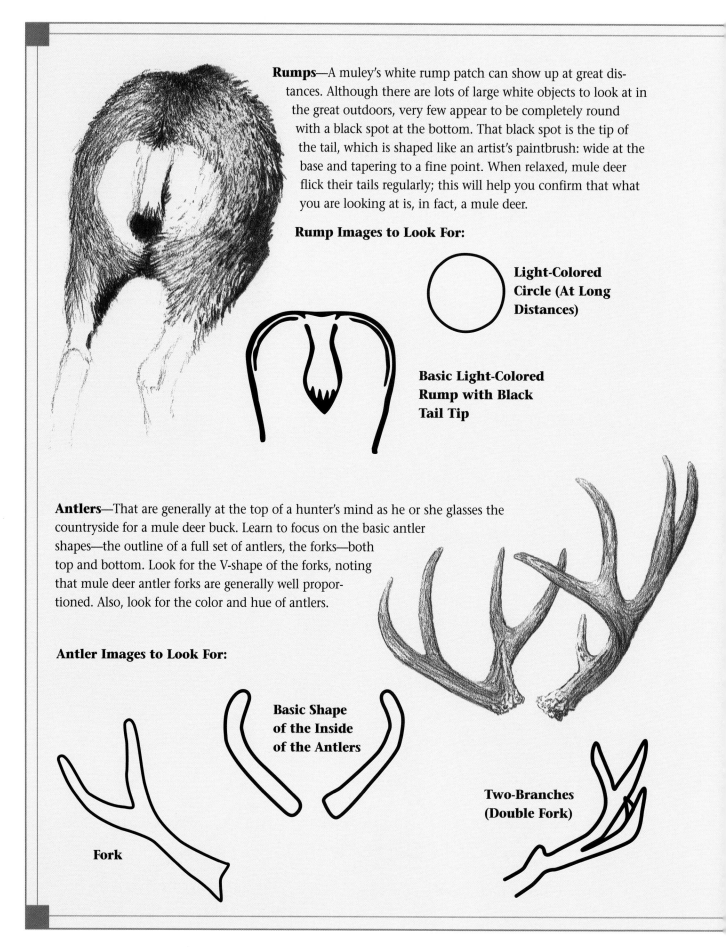

Rumps—A muley's white rump patch can show up at great distances. Although there are lots of large white objects to look at in the great outdoors, very few appear to be completely round with a black spot at the bottom. That black spot is the tip of the tail, which is shaped like an artist's paintbrush: wide at the base and tapering to a fine point. When relaxed, mule deer flick their tails regularly; this will help you confirm that what you are looking at is, in fact, a mule deer.

Rump Images to Look For:

Light-Colored Circle (At Long Distances)

Basic Light-Colored Rump with Black Tail Tip

Antlers—That are generally at the top of a hunter's mind as he or she glasses the countryside for a mule deer buck. Learn to focus on the basic antler shapes—the outline of a full set of antlers, the forks—both top and bottom. Look for the V-shape of the forks, noting that mule deer antler forks are generally well proportioned. Also, look for the color and hue of antlers.

Antler Images to Look For:

Basic Shape of the Inside of the Antlers

Two-Branches (Double Fork)

Fork

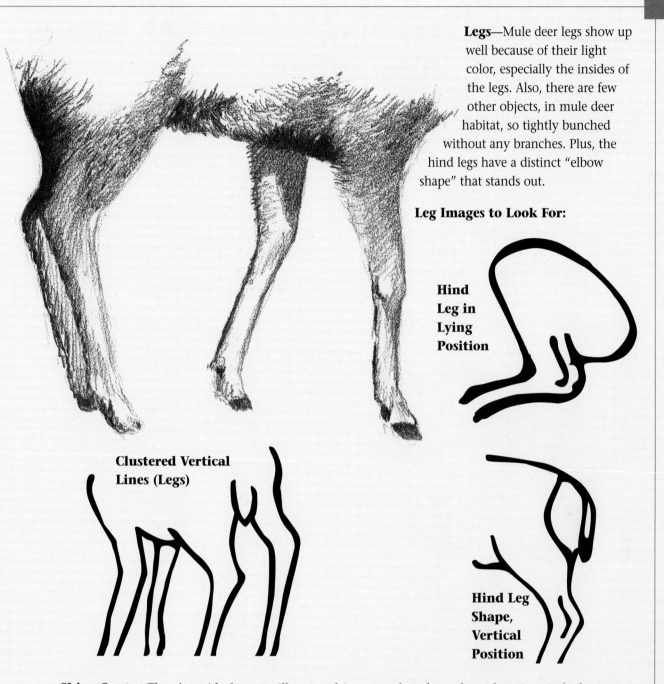

Legs—Mule deer legs show up well because of their light color, especially the insides of the legs. Also, there are few other objects, in mule deer habitat, so tightly bunched without any branches. Plus, the hind legs have a distinct "elbow shape" that stands out.

Leg Images to Look For:

Hind Leg in Lying Position

Clustered Vertical Lines (Legs)

Hind Leg Shape, Vertical Position

Shiny Spots—There's no ideal way to illustrate shiny spots, but always keep them in mind whenever you're trying to spot mule deer. Any one of the elements described (muzzle, ear, rump, antler, cocked leg, etc.) may first draw your attention simply as a shiny, different-looking spot. When you see something with a shine, sheen or different texture, stop and make your eyes investigate harder. You might be looking at a mule deer.

By memorizing these images—in the context of Faces, Ears, Rumps, Antlers and Legs, and to the point of blocking out all other landscape and foliage distractions—you will be surprised at how many more mule deer you will find, whether you're spot-and-stalk hunting, still-hunting, or even sitting on a stand.

TRACKING MULE DEER

When most folks think of mule deer hunting, they think about a classic spot-and-stalk hunt. They climb high before first light and let their eyes do the walking until they spot the buck they want, then make their move. Make no mistake, this is a great way to hunt mulies. But there's another way to get the job done, one that, when practiced with great skill and perseverance, just might be the best way to get a shot at a trophy-class buck. That method is tracking.

Tracking big game is, in many ways, a lost art. There is much more to it than simply cutting a track, taking it up, overtaking a buck and punching your tag. Much more. But in the right country, at the right time, taking up the track of an oversized buck that lives virtually all his life at night just might be your only chance to take him.

WHERE TRACKING WORKS

Generally speaking, high-country mule deer hunters are not trackers per se. The country is too big, the canyons too deep, the ground too hard and the deer too scattered. Tracking is most productive in lower-elevation country, where it's flatter and the ground is easier to read. Two general areas and types of terrain that come immediately to mind are the pinion/juniper country in places like southern Utah and northern Arizona; the thick oakbrush hillsides in northwestern Colorado; and the deserts of southern California, Arizona, New Mexico and Sonora, Mexico.

Tracking is the classic way to hunt desert mule deer. I've been on a half-dozen hunts down into Sonora, Mexico, and spent hundreds of hours looking for tracks. I've been fortunate enough to have been taught some of the tricks of the trade by some superb Mexican trackers, and I have taken my two largest mule deer this way. It is often frustrating, always demanding, but never boring.

Pinion/juniper country produces some of the largest bucks taken these days. Why? In this relatively flat, incredibly thick terrain, spotting and stalking good bucks is extremely difficult, if not impossible. When taken in this region, it is often on a late-season, limited-entry permit that allows some hunting during the initial stages of the rut, which pulls the bucks out of the thick cover and out onto more open sagebrush flats. General rifle season hunters often are forced to go into the thick stuff and root the bucks out. That's where the skilled tracker can really shine.

The other time tracking works very well is after the

Tracking up a big mule deer buck is one of the most exciting—and difficult—challenges I've ever undertaken. The deserts of the southwestern U.S. and northern Mexico are a great place to track muleys.

snow flies. In fact, the best time to track mule deer bucks is right after a fresh snowfall, for two reasons: It is easy to age tracks, and the deer are unusually active. And obviously, locating and following tracks in snow is much easier than finding and staying on them in rocky, dry ground. However, tracking in snow is anything but a no-brainer. In both snow country and the low elevations, you must know how to read tracks, and how to work them. And you must be fit enough to stay on them for hours.

HOW TO TRACK

Obviously, you first have to find a track to follow. Those familiar with their hunting area and/or those who have spent some time scouting will have an idea of where the deer are, where they've seen bucks in previous trips and so on. The time of year, current weather conditions and hunting pressure are all factors that determine where the deer are at any given time. For example, in dry conditions water sources are magnets for mule deer of all sizes and both sexes.

Sometimes, though, you just stumble across a track. This is often the case when I find a big buck track. I

The first morning after a fresh snow is the best time of all to track up a buck. It is easy to age tracks now, and since deer are unusually active following a heavy snow, it is relatively easy to find a fresh track to follow.

A tracker's dream—a monster buck in his bed, undisturbed and without a care in the world. Can you keep it together long enough to make the shot, or will this dream buck bolt and be gone forever?

am hunting an area I know has some big deer (my pre-hunt research and scouting led me here for that very reason), and during the course of the hunt I find a big track.

The first step is to evaluate that track. Buck or doe? Fresh or old? (The sidebar on page 101 lists some of the key things to look for.) I also visualize the country—using my past experiences, topographic maps and what I see at the moment—and factor in weather and season. Now my mind is racing ahead, anticipating what the buck is doing and where he's going. My first thought is to find the nearest rough country—a thick, inaccessible hellhole he might use as a bedding area. If everything is right—wind direction, track size, freshness—and soon it's time to begin the hunt. But before I do, I study the track closely. Are there any unique characteristics to that track that will help me recognize it if it happens to become jumbled with others later? Look for unique shapes or irregularities to the track. I like to take my quarter-inch tape measure and measure both length and width, which can help me identify it later.

As you track the deer, it is critical to keep your senses on red alert from the beginning. Squirrels scamper and birds flutter on the edge of the woods, suddenly sending a shock-charge of adrenaline through you. Rocks, blow-downs and shadows take on the shape of deer backs and antler tines. Even though they probably are inanimate objects, all must be investigated. The one time you don't investigate is the time that deer-shaped tree trunk will explode from its bed. Guaranteed.

Whenever possible, I try to stay off to the side when tracking a deer; I don't follow directly on the track itself. Mature bucks have habits of watching their backside as they move and bedding down for the day where they can observe anything following them. I also never rivet all my attention to the tracks. Instead I am constantly scanning ahead, looking for a piece of a deer or movement. By assessing the lay of the land, it is relatively easy to anticipate which way the deer traveled. It also helps you determine whether he is traveling fast or slow.

For example, when his tracks run relatively straight and the prints are placed well apart, the buck is covering some ground. He's probably moving from a feeding area to his bedding area. Now I move as quickly as I can, remembering the importance of stealth, wind direction and watching ahead.

However, when the tracks begin to weave and meander and the length of the deer's stride begins to shorten, it's time to slow way down and do some hard looking. This type of trail generally means the buck is looking for a place to bed down. Mature bucks are very aware of the danger their tracks put them in—especially in snow—and, more often than not, will swing a wide circle and double back a bit before bedding. It's very important to scan—not just the trail ahead, but off to the sides as well. Often when you

Is there a muley hunter alive who doesn't get the shakes when he stumbles across a huge buck track?

Mule Deer—Western Challenge

spot the deer, it will be to the side of the tracks you can see. At this point, tracking becomes just as much a game of still-hunting as anything else.

I SPOOKED HIM; NOW WHAT?

Tracking mule deer is not easy. Anyone who does much tracking knows that you end up either never finding the deer—the trail is too long for the available daylight, the tracks simply petered out into nothing or a million and one assorted gremlins help you lose the trail—or you spook the buck and never see him. It's happened to me a bazillion times. Here's what I do.

If I blow a buck out and he's close, but the cover is so thick I can't see him, I immediately run after him as fast as I can. I know I can't outrun a mule deer. But what I'm hoping is that I'll get lucky and catch a glimpse of him as he bounds across an open sage flat, or even better, races up the opposite canyon wall. When I run through the thick brush and reach an open area where I can see well, I stop, sit down, and both

look and listen hard. I've killed several bucks this way.

It's also important to remember that the biggest muley bucks are unlikely to bound across open areas because if they had a tendency to, they would have been killed long ago. If you spook a big buck today, more than likely he's going to hide and let you go by him. I've seen it happen a lot, both to others and to me. The deer blows out of his bed, plunges off a steep canyon wall, then after a short ways circles back into a patch of thick stuff and lies down as he waits for danger to simply walk away.

Often, though, it's just too thick or the buck circles me back into the nasty cover, and I can't see him. At this point most hunters give up the chase and try to find another deer to hunt. That's sound advice. If he doesn't hide to let you past, he'll often run for miles and stay alert for hours. A spooked muley buck— especially a mature buck that has survived several hunting seasons—is going to be wired up and almost impossible to catch.

That's not always the case, though. One time in

When tracking muleys, you're going to spook a lot of deer. Don't panic though. Assess the situation and keep the hunt going. And don't be surprised if the buck doesn't run far, but instead circles you and dives into the thickest cover around to try and hide.

How to Hunt Mule Deer

With the help of Antonio Aguiar, a superb Mexican tracker, I tracked up this huge desert muley in Sonora, Mexico, and shot him at 70 yards without him knowing we were on the planet. The 16-pointer has an outside spread of 34 inches and scores 243 Boone & Crockett points—despite having broken off two long tines.

northern Arizona, I jumped a good buck in the thick stuff. I glimpsed his antlers as he barrelled through a small opening without giving me a shot, and I wanted him. It was an hour after daylight, so I sat down and waited an hour, then took up the track. At first it was obvious where the deer went—the long strides and deep tracks of a running buck were easy to find. After about a mile, though, he slowed to a walk. I followed these tracks for a bit, then made a decision.

Many times, mature bucks that know you're on their trail simply won't stop walking. They don't move quickly, but they never slow down. Often, they move in a large figure-eight pattern. They don't want to leave the security of their home range, and so rather than travel for miles and miles in a straight line, they'll figure-eight until they're back home and have lost that troublesome tracker.

In one such situation I had to decide whether or not the buck swung left or right in his figure-eight. I chose right, which that day was to the north. So I took a compass reading, then started hiking at a 90-degree

angle, or east, away from the deer's trail. After a mile, I slowly swung back to the north. Thirty minutes later I cut his track, easily identifiable by the deformed toe on his left foot. Man, my heart beat like a jackhammer! The deer walked normally now and I once again trailed him. I never shot that buck, because his tracks led into a large area of hard rock, where I lost them. But the day sure was exciting, and I learned a lot.

MY BIGGEST BUCK EVER

The same thing happened one rainy day in Sonora, Mexico. My guide and I jumped five deer in the thick desert brush; three does and two bucks. We knew some really huge deer lived in this area, and chose to follow the largest track and a single doe. This deer also had a deformed toe.

Two hours later we knew we had to roll the dice, leave his trail and gamble that we could pick it up later, or we'd never catch that deer. This we did, and 45 minutes later we came across his track again. We both smiled at each other and continued the hunt.

The tracks led into some very thick stuff. The buck was still with his doe—it was January, during the rut in this area—and we were on pins and needles. By and by we came to an open lane, with visibility for 75 yards. Standing there was a brown animal, but as I threw my .280 up it turned into a wild-eyed range cow. The deer's tracks led right under his belly. Oh man, I remember thinking, please don't spook and run now!

Suddenly, from behind a large thornbush directly behind that cow came the buck, walking left to right with no clue about our presence. It was all over in a second, and soon I admired the largest buck of my life. He had an outside spread of 34½ inches, 16 scorable points, and despite the fact that he broke off a long rear point on the left antler and his right eye guard, still scores 243 Boone and Crockett points.

Tracking deer is not for everyone. It's not easy, and often not productive. And yet, it just might be the best way for you to take your largest buck.

After that Sonoran adventure, how could I be anything but a believer?

Reading Tracks

When you come across a deer track, can you tell how old it is? Whether it was made by a buck or doe? What the deer was doing? Here are some tips on reading tracks:

Gait. Rather than planting one foot in front of the other, a buck usually has a gait that shows a pronounced outward kick of his feet. It appears as if he is walking crow-footed, and the trail often looks as if it were made by a drunken sailor. Does and fawns generally walk in a more straight line.

Drag. Small deer tend to take high steps, lifting their hooves clear of soft soil and snow with each step. Heavy-bodied deer—bucks—tend to drag their hooves, often carving clefts in the snow or soft dirt between tracks.

Size. Large deer have large feet. While this is an unreliable indicator, if you see lots of deer tracks in an area and suddenly come across a set of tracks that are markedly larger than the others you've seen, you almost can be sure that a big-bodied buck made them. In soft soil, a buck's heavy body sinks into the earth and may leave dew claw prints.

Age. Determining track age is difficult and dependent on many factors—like soil or snow conditions and whether or not it has rained recently. Experience is the best way to learn about track age. Generally speaking, though, fresh tracks are sharply defined. They have definite edges. The older they get, the more they lose this definition.

Single set. Bucks like to travel alone. Even during the rut when they're trailing does, they usually do so off to the side of the doe/fawn tracks. When I see a big set of single tracks, I begin to get excited. This could very well be the big ol' buck of my dreams.

HUNTING THE RUT

Whitetail hunters believe that hunting the rut is a magical time, when they have their best chance of the entire season to take a mature buck. Generally, this thinking is right on the money. When the breeding urge takes over, caution is often thrown to the wind, because even the most secretive buck has no choice but to answer nature's call.

While you can find a library full of information dealing with rut-hunt tactics for whitetails, there is little available on the importance of hunting the rut for mule deer and its coastal cousin, the Columbian blacktail. Is that because hunting during the breeding season is a less effective way to locate, and harvest, mature bucks of these two deer species?

Not on your life. Just as it is when hunting big whitetails, the mule deer rut can be your best chance of the year to take the buck of your dreams.

MULE DEER RUT BEHAVIOR

The rutting season occurs during late fall. Depending on the latitude of the deer, this is anytime from early November to late December and January. When planning a rut hunt for mulies and blacktails in new country, it pays to call area biologists to determine when the rut generally occurs and when the peak of the rut is anticipated.

Like whitetails, during courtship a mule deer buck tests a doe's readiness for breeding by obtaining a urine sample. According to noted biologist and author, Dr. Valerius Geist, mule deer are the only ungulates who have two methods of obtaining this urine sample. They do this by the familiar "low stretch" approach, where the buck

Trailing a herd of does during the rut is a great way to locate a good buck that will eventually show up.

nates, at which time the buck moves in and "lip-curls" to determine the doe's readiness for breeding.

The second method occurs when the buck becomes impatient as he waits for the doe to urinate. When this occurs, he may throw what Dr. Geist describes as a "temper tantrum." Then with little notice, his body becomes stiff, his upper lip begins to quiver, and a high-pitched tone resonates from deep within his throat. The buck may then throw himself, antlers lowered, at the courted female, all the while roaring. When she takes off he follows right on her heels, slams the ground with his front legs and bellows with every jump. After a couple hundred yards, this chase usually ends with the buck resuming the low stretch position, and the female usually urinating.

During the rut mule deer herds exhibit a characteristic more commonly associated with elk. The does, badgered by every testosterone-overloaded juvenile buck in the region, often stay close to the dominant buck and seek his protection from unwanted advances. The smaller bucks often circle the herd, just like young "satellite" elk bulls, waiting for their chance to sneak in and satisfy their breeding urge. The difference between elk and mule deer is that the dominant buck does not control the does like a bull elk

approaches the female from behind in a low stretched posture, licking his nose and uttering soft calls, not unlike a fawn distress call. He may then touch the female with his muzzle. The female acts as if she is ignoring him, feeding and moving in small half circles. The courtship continues until the female urinates

As is the case with all deer hunting, the rut is the one time during the year when wise old monster bucks throw caution to the wind and become very vulnerable to hunters. Serious trophy muley hunters plan their entire year around the muley rut.

How to Hunt Mule Deer

When the rut is combined with a fresh snowfall, you should be able to locate the tracks of large bucks as they roam the country looking for does in estrus.

controls a harem of cows. Instead, he is interested in one specific doe at a time, which is the one in, or closest to, estrus; he's just hanging out with the ladies.

When a buck and a doe breed, they usually are isolated from the larger group of does for a day or two. The doe's estrus period lasts about a day, during which time she repeatedly breeds with a buck. Naturally, smaller bucks crisscrossing the range looking for does may come upon the pair, in which case they try to split them up so that they can do some breeding too.

The bulk of the mule deer rut lasts three to four weeks. During this time the older breeding bucks lose much of their physical strength, often breaking antler points and receiving tears in their coats from fighting, and appearing listless and dazed near the end of the cycle. When they quit breeding—they often quit cold turkey in one day—they become isolated, looking for thick bedding cover in which they can recuperate enough strength to survive the winter. Post-rut behavior sees bucks disperse, rest for about three or four weeks,

then emerge when it's near time to shed their antlers and battle winter. They often join doe herds at this time, seeking the security from predators that large numbers of animals brings.

BASIC RUT HUNT TACTICS

During the rut, mature mule deer bucks lose much of the caution that dominates their lives during the rest of the year. Bucks that wouldn't think of being caught out in the open and away from the dark timber or thick brush in which they live during daylight hours, now are seen moving across open sage flats and bare hillsides searching for does in estrus.

Hunters can use a buck's behavior to their advantage in several ways. In open and semi-open terrain, the best technique is to climb to a high vantage point and carefully glass the surrounding countryside for deer. This is true for both mule deer and blacktails. Once a herd of does—at this time of year, they're like a buck magnet—is located, take your time and glass both the herd and the surrounding hills for a buck. If you don't spot a buck right away, don't despair. He may be isolated and breeding with a doe in a nearby coulee or thicket. I remember one Utah muzzleloader hunt in November in which my partner and I checked on a herd of two dozen does every day for a week until finally, the day before we were to head home, a dandy buck appeared in their midst. Good things, as they say, often come to those who wait.

When in estrus, a muley doe may breed with a buck several times to ensure she is impregnated. The bulk of the mule deer rut lasts about 3 to 4 weeks.

When a buck and doe breed, they often remain together for a day or so before the buck heads out to find another mate. Bucks will hang with or near doe herds at this time, waiting for a single doe to come into estrus.

If you spot only fair-to-middlin' bucks with the does, don't give up. I once drew a special tag for a December hunt in California's eastern Sierra Nevada Mountains. On the first day my friend Jim Matthews and I spotted a herd of deer high on the mountain, in which there were a pair of good bucks. I left them alone, hoping a *really* big buck would come along and take over. I checked on them every other day until the last day of the season, when I decided that the larger of the pair would do. I climbed the 1,500-foot slope in the dark, and when dawn broke and I could see the deer, I was rewarded instead with the *really* big buck I had hoped for. When I shot him that frigid morning—it was so cold and windy my camera froze, and I didn't get a single picture—I found that two of the three small cheaters he was carrying earlier in the week were broken off while sparring. It was a

Lots of rutting takes place on lower-altitude, private land. Ask permission and you might get access.

great hunt, and a no-lose situation for me. If the big buck hadn't come along, as often happens, I'd have been in the chips anyway. As it was, I took my largest California buck in over 20 years of annual hunting.

It should be noted that much rut behavior occurs on or near the winter range. This lower-elevation terrain can be everything from sagebrush flats to cedar and juniper jungles, to open hillsides or privately owned crop lands. Learning where this winter range is—and therefore, where the deer are likely to be—prior to hunting is important to your success.

If the deer are on private land, obtaining permission to hunt is vital. If permission is not possible, you can often hunt those deer off the private ground and on public land, when the deer sometimes go to bed in brushy draws and hillsides. I shot a big buck with my bow one year in New Mexico out of a large herd

How to Hunt Mule Deer

of deer that followed a set routine every day. The deer fed in an alfalfa field at dawn and lingered there for a couple of hours before departing the private ground and moving to adjacent juniper and brush-covered public land hills to bed for the day. I laid ambush after ambush for that buck, only to be busted by one of his 40-some companions for seven straight days. A light snow dusted the ground on the eighth day, when I found them bedded in the junipers. I slowly sneaked within 45 yards of the bedded deer and grunted the buck to his feet and 20 yards closer before my arrow found its mark.

That brings us to the next phase of rut hunting—calling.

One of the best ways to take a big blacktail buck is by rattling and grunting during the rut. I've had some success grunting up muleys too, but not nearly as much as with blacktails.

CALLING MULIES & BLACKTAILS

Calling whitetails by using either vocal sounds or rattling has been an accepted technique for many years. Yet many hunters are still amazed that you can do the same thing with mulies and blacktails.

And why not? All deer species are vocal, emitting grunts, squeaks and squeals at varying times. Mulies and blacktails will lock horns and battle like it was Superbowl Sunday during the rut. They'll also rake their antlers on small conifers, cedars and junipers, as well as engage in mock battle with brush. And just like calling whitetails, hunters must pick the time and place to use calling techniques. The rut is that time.

One of the best techniques for taking those big, super sleuth blacktail bucks that live in the Pacific Northwest's rain forest jungles is to rattle them in during the rut. Many of these hunts are restricted to archery and blackpowder weapons, but in the heavy cover these deer live in and in which you must hunt, shots generally are short. I have several friends who like to hike or drive along logging roads looking for fresh deer sign late in the season. Once they find it, they hike around looking for more. When they find an area of high activity, they hike along, set a portable tree-stand, then rattle and grunt. The treestand allows them to see down into the thick cover, making it easier to find a buck than if they were trying to do the same thing from ground level. They'll stay in one place for 30 minutes to an hour, then move.

Mule deer also respond, on occasion, to rattling, as well as grunting and the low pitch of a fawn distress call, which sounds, as we learned earlier, a lot like a large buck following a doe that he is encouraging to urinate.

I've found that both rattling and calling work best in relatively thick cover, which can be anything from thick timber stands, to deep brushy canyons and draws, to coastal rain forest fauna. In open country, like sagebrush flatlands, I've had little success with rattling and virtually none with calling, unless it is to a buck I already spotted and stalked near. With mule deer, my own pre-ferred method is to spot them before they see me and stalk in for a shot. But calling and rattling worked for me when I was not able to locate deer living in the thick stuff. It's worth considering—even though both are "whitetail" tactics.

The mule deer rut is a magical time, especially for mule deer hunters. It's not a time for freezer hunting, though, of course, the delicious meat is a welcome addition to the larder. Instead, it's a time to observe the deer and learn about them. It's also a time to hold out for the buck of your life. There's no better time to find him than right now!

Late-season blacktail rut hunters who set treestands near known doe pockets have good success.

Where to Hunt Rutting Mulies

More and more states are making the mule deer rut hunt a special-draw type of hunt only, as they should. Increasing pressure on mule deer from many fronts—including habitat loss, hunting pressure, increasing elk herds and increasing loss to predators (like coyotes and mountain lions)—has put mule deer populations on the edge.

Montana is one exception to the special-draw rut hunt rule, as it continues to permit rut hunting on a general buck tag, with the rifle season lasting through Thanksgiving weekend. Another state with excellent trophy potential, Arizona, requires either a special-draw tag or archery-only hunting during the rut; both mulies and Coues' deer rut in January there, and archery licenses can be obtained for both species over-the-counter. The season for the giant desert mulies of Sonora, Mexico, runs from mid-December through mid-January, which is prime rutting time. In Oregon, your best chance at a huge Columbia blacktail is during the November rut, when hunting is restricted to those who have drawn limited-entry muzzleloader or archery tags.

If a big muley or blacktail buck is your goal, researching potential rut-hunt options makes a lot of sense. Obtain copies of state game regulations, research potential areas, then apply for special-draw tags when necessary. Doing so tips the odds of spotting the largest buck you've ever seen heavily in your favor.

IN THE DRIVER'S SEAT

Driving game was perhaps the first method of hunting. History books tell us of Native Americans' preference for driving bison over cliffs in Montana, of tireless runners doggedly driving game for days at a time into carefully select-ed natural traps and other forms of drive-type hunting. Driving can be a very effective way of hunting mule deer even today, though most look upon it more as a social event, a way to fill the freezer more than as a serious way to hunt trophy-class bucks, or

a method of last resort.

That's not to say that there aren't deer drives carried out with all the forethought and precision of a military campaign. There are, and these are, by far, the most successful of their kind.

MAKING THE DEER MOVE

One time in Spain, I was part of what the Spaniards call a "monteria." This is a wild game drive across a large piece of property, in which riflemen are set at intervals of 100 to 200 yards on knolls overlooking a fair amount of country. The drivers use truckloads of dogs of all shapes, sizes and colors, most of questionable breeding, many of which were taken from the local pound the day before. The drivers and dogs make an incredible racket as they roust through the brush, pushing ahead of them myriad animals, including wild boars, red stags, fallow deer, mouflon sheep and small game like rabbits.

The game came racing past our stands, breathless with tongues hanging out, and dashed across the open country. Our instructions were simple: Shoot anything and everything, except the gold medal (trophy-class) stags and rams. It was an experience I'll never forget, but the shooting was challenging, to say the least.

In North America, the most successful drives are done in a much more refined manner. Deer that are walking slowly or at a slow trot, stopping periodically to pause, are a much better target than those wild-eyed, racing Spanish animals.

One of the real keys to a successful deer drive is to get the deer up and moving in as natural a manner as possible. The end result is that they move where you want them to go—not where they prefer to go. One of the big reasons most drives fail is that the drivers move too quickly and noisily through the countryside. You simply can't move deer in a controlled manner when moving at too fast a pace. And eliminate the talking. In my experience, the slower and quieter the approach, the better. When drivers move too rapidly, they have little chance of guiding the deer along.

Another reason for driving quietly is that, if unsuccessful, once the drive is over you want the deer

Driving game was one of man's earliest hunting methods. Modern mule deer hunters can successfully drive bucks to the gun too.

to return to the area and use it again. Driving noisily, or too frequently, will move many of the deer out of the area completely, or turn them nocturnal. Often the larger bucks will be gone for good. By taking a walk in the woods and not raising too much Cain, the chances are very good that you'll be able to hunt the driven area again with good results in a few days.

PLANNING SUCCESSFUL DRIVES

The best drives, as mentioned earlier, are those conducted with much forethought and planning, just like a military campaign. Planning should be based on scouting. It's much easier for someone familiar with a piece of ground and with the area's deer to plan a successful drive, than someone who is visiting for the first time.

The premise that deer follow natural lines of cover

or terrain when under pressure is a sound one on which to base any drive. Points, long fingers of timber, creekbottoms, finger ridges, the edges of ponds and lakes, saddles, the edge of thick cover, deep canyons, an "edge" where thin brush meets heavier brush ... all are good directors of deer. Smart drives are built to direct the game's movements into these natural funnels, where standers lie in ambush.

One of the most important things in setting up a drive is making sure that when the team leader directs a person to a specific stand in a specific spot, that the shooter *stays there*. Often, the better bucks catch a faint whiff of human scent or a slight sound, and they move ahead first. Your best chance for taking these bucks is during the first few minutes of a drive hunt. And, as mentioned earlier, deer will often sneak back through the drivers, creating shot opportunities long after they've passed.

Mule Deer—Western Challenge

I know one western rancher who lives adjacent to a wide, shallow river dotted with small islands, overgrown with thick brush and a few mature conifers. For years he saw good bucks swim out and live on a couple of these islands after hunting pressure pushed them off the mainland riverbottoms.

He tried still-hunting these deer for a while, but it never did any good. Then he set treestands, but he still didn't get any shots. The next year he figured he had it whipped. The islands were small, so he got a bunch of friends together and drove the deer in one massive swoop. But when that didn't produce any shots either, he didn't quite know what to do. He knew the deer were still there—there were fresh droppings, tracks and beds scattered everywhere. But how to get a shot?

Then it dawned on him. The cover was so thick, the bucks were simply sneaking back through the drivers and making a clean getaway. So the next time, he decided to get sneaky too.

Before the season he preset a few treestands along heavily used trails in the middle of the thickest brush, so the bucks would get used to them. When it was time to drive the deer, he set everything up as he normally did—drivers coming in from upwind, with standers near the end of the island in ground blinds. But this time he had the drivers work in pairs. As they snuck through the brush and reached the preset stands, one climbed up and got ready, while the other continued. He hoped the deer couldn't count, figuring that by having one man proceed, the deer would never know that a shooter had slipped into a stand. On that first hunt, two of the three backdoor standers each shot a dandy buck doing what it had done for years—circling the drivers back to its favorite brush patch.

The size of the land mass being hunted dictates the number of people necessary to drive it successfully. The larger the land mass, the more people you need to get the job done. But selecting a land mass that is overly large works against you. In my experience, hunters often bite off way more than they can chew when they're trying to drive deer. It's usually better to scale things down and drive smaller pieces of ground that can be worked thoroughly in a relatively short period of time, giving the deer fewer chances to slip back through the drivers. These smaller parcels are also easier for the hunt master to place each driver and stander precisely, a key to moving deer where he wants them to go, not where they would rather travel. In fact, two-person mini-drives

The key to successful drive hunting is planning. Having a planner who knows both the lay of the land and how the deer like to move across it will up the odds of a success immeasurably.

Before beginning a drive, it is helpful to show all the participants a map of the area being driven, and how the drive is expected to work. This will keep everyone focused on their assigned job.

knowledge of the land and prevailing wind, as well as knowledge of the deer and their habits. Another old cliché, "Too many cooks spoil the broth," fits deer driving. Only well-coordinated drives, in which everyone is thinking alike and working together, will produce consistent success.

Topographic maps are also important tools when planning deer drives. These maps show obvious potential funnels, and help the hunt master coordinate his plan. They also help those less familiar with the land mass being hunted to get a feel for the country, as well as show them where roads and property boundaries lie. One of my friends has several topo maps of his favorite hunting area, over which he's placed a clear sheet of lightweight plastic. On the plastic he uses a grease pencil to outline his drives, as well as to mark stand locations, known deer bedding areas and funnels, prevailing wind directions and more. Using these maps helps him get a clear picture of what needs to be done given prevailing weather conditions, hunter numbers and so on. His drives almost always produce action.

can sometimes be the best drives of all.

When two hunting partners who think alike team up, they can be a hard combination to beat. Often one of my good hunting partners and I will take turns driving minuscule patches of cover, usually working the deer down toward the heads of cuts and draws, or along the edges of hills, fences or creeks. By knowing the terrain and playing the wind, it's possible to move a handful of deer at a time through a narrow funnel, creating a shot opportunity for the lone stander.

I've mentioned the "hunt master" frequently. It's important when planning a deer drive to have one person in charge. This person should have an intimate

THE DRAG LINE

A good mule deer driving technique is what I call the "drag line." This seems to work better in slightly open woods, as opposed to really thick cover, from which it can be almost impossible to move the deer. Here's how it works:

Set the drive line as you normally would, with the drivers in a relatively straight line, reasonably close together—but not too close. Set standers as normal, and begin the drive. But this time, have one or two hunters stay well behind the main group of pushers, moving at a snail's pace and keeping off main deer trails, preferably staying next to any cover available. This works best in a crosswind, or on days when the wind is squirrely and unpredictable. It is also a good idea for the drag line hunters to stop and sit for several minutes at a time.

Paralleling the trails keeps the wind from busting you. Moving slowly keeps you well back of the pushers and gives you time to look and glass ahead constantly for the sign of a deer that has slipped through the line and is trying to escape through the back door. If you work it right, you'll be amazed at the number of deer you see when working the drag line. If the truth be known, it's my favorite place in a driving scheme, even more so than taking a stand set in a known funnel. If given the choice, I'll take drag line duty every time! I've used the drag line technique successfully in thick oak brush and mountain mahogany stands, as well as in brushy stands of aspens.

CROSS-CANYON DRIVES

The most popular mule deer drive is to have two to four hunters divide their forces and work a deep, brushy draw or canyon from the top down. The hunters stay within sight of each other and walk banging the brush and throwing rocks into thick cover as they go, working their way along the canyon walls to the bottom, where hopefully some standers are covering the exits.

On this drive, the pushers need to be alert both for deer literally jumping out from beneath their feet, and

A great source for discovering the whereabouts of mulies and their escape routes: ranchers, property owners and other people close to the land.

the sight of deer moving ahead of the pushers across the canyon. These are common ways to get a shot.

SPOT 'EM FIRST

One very successful method of taking bucks—often, better than average bucks—is first to spot the deer bedded. The best thing that can happen, of course, is

How to Hunt Mule Deer

"Soft" Drives Are the Key

When driving mule deer it's important to drive the deer "softly." That simply means to get the deer moving without panicking them into a gallop. When deer are running full-bore in panic, you may see a deer from your stand, but the chances of getting a quality shot are poor.

To do this, begin the drive by setting standers well ahead of time in known funnels with the wind blowing from drivers to standers. The drivers must begin their move by simply walking slowly through the cover, not "driving" per se. The drivers are spaced relatively close together, but not too close, the exact spacing dependent on the thickness of the cover and overall size of the land mass being driven. You don't want the deer to slip back through the drive line, which they may try to do.

Often it is best if the drivers move relatively silently, sneaking through the woods and actually still-hunting the deer. Of course, this rarely is successful, especially when the drive is set up with the wind in favor of the standers. But that's the point. By allowing the scent and sound of the approaching drivers to softly float to the deer, the animals will often be up and moving well ahead of their perceived enemies.

The key is for the drivers to thoroughly work the area, and in no great hurry. In thick cover, once the drivers move past the standers, it's a good idea for the standers to remain on station for 30 to 45 minutes after the drivers walk out of sight. Every now and then, a sneaky deer tries to slip back through the drive line into its core area, especially if the drive pushed them to its edge. When they do, those still on stand just might get a shot.

then to move in and shoot. But sometimes the deer are bedded in places where getting close enough for a shot is darn near impossible. Then, setting up a short drive can produce success.

This is where a knowledge of local deer habits and the lay of the land can pay big dividends. I like to position the standers downwind of the deer in natural escape funnels or along the edges of thick cover. They may be posted anywhere between a half-mile and a mile away, and may not be able to see the deer once they move into position (which they must do silently and out of sight of the deer). The pushers then stalk the buck, keeping in mind that one of their goals is to move the deer to the standers. The standers stay alert and ready, of course, but also remain out of sight until it's time to shoot.

Driving mule deer isn't as popular as working the whitetail woods back east. Some spot-and-stalk purists frown on driving as a waste of time. And yet, when all else fails, a well-executed drive can put meat in the freezer and antlers on the wall. And among all the other glories of mule deer country, that's one reason for being out there.

The key to driving mulies is to get the deer up and moving as naturally as possible, and not scaring them into running wild. Spotting a bedded buck first, then trying to move him to strategically positioned standers, is the best drive of all.

How to Hunt Mule Deer

Chapter 5

THE BLACKTAIL COAST

Most hunters know very little about black-tailed deer. And yet, while mule deer are still the West's most popular big game animal, there are three states—Washington, Oregon and California—where the Columbia blacktail is now drawing the lion's share of attention from deer hunters. And in Alaska, where the Sitka blacktail is the only deer available, both residents and nonresidents hunt them vigorously.

Like the deer themselves, The Blacktail Coast is a secretive place. Dominated by dense, seemingly impenetrable old-growth forests from northern California through coastal British Columbia and the Alaska panhandle, deer hunters can have trouble just walking through the thick stuff, let alone finding a buck to hunt. Farther south, from below San Francisco Bay to the blacktail's boundary in central California, the public land is defined by vast tracts of national forest land covered with brush so thick you sometimes have to crawl under it to get around.

In this thick cover blacktails have learned to live a secretive life. Their home range is small—though some blacktail herds are migratory—and the bucks move very little, if at all, during daylight hours. Such conditions and activity levels—or lack of—create the need for unique hunting tactics and techniques to be successful.

There are few big game animals in all of North America more difficult to tie your tag on than a mature Columbia blacktail buck. If you think of yourself as an A-1, highly skilled buck hunter, take the blacktail challenge. I'll make you a little bet, right here and now. When you do, you will be humbled like you never thought possible. You'll walk away shaking your head, wondering how in the world such a small package could make such a big fool out of you.

But I warn you. Don't take the challenge if you can't handle another addiction. Because blacktail hunting is addicting. The challenge is so great, and the rewards so sweet that when success finally comes, you'll find yourself applying for another tag, ready to prove that the first time wasn't a fluke.

Blacktail hunting. It will get under your skin. Don't you wish it were time to go right now?

COLUMBIA BLACKTAILS

Columbia blacktails often are called the "Pacific Ghost." With few exceptions—Alaska's lightly hunted Sitka blacktails and low-pressure Lower 48 private land Columbia blacktails—these secretive deer spend their lives ghosting invisibly through the old-growth timber and coastal rain forest jungles from central California north to Alaska. Blacktails are a mule deer subspecies, but they live more like whitetails. They often have a relatively small home range, and the bigger bucks rarely expose themselves outside their thick cover homes except— like whitetails—during the rut.

After extensively hunting all North American deer species from coast to coast, north to south, I find that, for me, taking a trophy-class Columbia blacktail is the most difficult deer hunting task of all. I grew up in California, and have hunted Columbia black- tails since I was in high school. Yet 30 years later— after countless days chasing them throughout their range—I still find the deer supremely challenging, the hunting incredibly exciting. And for pure fun and lots of action, hunting Alaska's Sitka blacktails simply can't be beat. With blacktails, there's some- thing for everyone.

Just how tough are mature blacktails to take? A study by the Oregon Department of Fish and Game used infrared trail timer devices with cameras mount- ed on them to track several hundred blacktails as they moved down heavily used migration trails during hunting season. The timers recorded deer passing by

both day and night and photographed virtually all of them. This study told researchers that almost 87 percent of mature blacktail bucks—that's seven out of eight deer more than $2^1/_2$ years old—never moved during legal shooting hours. These deer remained inside their jungle hellholes, where they are invulnerable except to the most persistent and skilled—or the luckiest—hunters.

HABITAT AREA DESCRIPTIONS

Depending on where they live, Columbia blacktails occupy widely varied terrain, from the oak/grassland foothills of central California to the rain forest jungles of coastal Oregon and British Columbia. The techniques used to hunt them successfully are based on this habitat. In the thick rain forests, still-hunting and setting treestands are highly effective. Oak/grassland country lends itself to spot-and-stalk hunting. During the rut—when firearms tags are issued by special-draw only and are hard to get—rattling and grunting can work.

To understand how to hunt blacktails, you must first know where they live, and adjust your tactics and technique accordingly. Here's where to find them.

Most Columbia blacktail country is steep, with plenty of thick timber.

COASTAL BRITISH COLUMBIA

This region is an extension of southeast Alaska in terms of habitat and hunting style and technique. Good deer hunting is found on the mainland, but the best known and most popular area—at least with nonresidents—is Vancouver Island. Deer here are classified as Columbia blacktails, except those on the Queen Charlotte Islands, which are classified as Sitka blacktails. While deer numbers are good, trophy quality is just fair when compared to the coastal U.S. The largest three British Columbia bucks listed in the 10th edition

of the Boone and Crockett Club's *Records of North American Big Game* from this area are ranked numbers 63, 73 and 159.

PACIFIC NORTHWEST

The rain forest jungles of coastal Washington and northern Oregon hold good numbers of Columbia blacktails, and some really big bucks. This thick, wet country is often coursed by still-hunters who use logging roads for access, then poke along on foot. The best jungle hunters I know approach the game like an eastern whitetail hunter, scouting for sign, then setting treestands and ground blinds in the hopes of ambushing a deer. Calling—both vocally and with rattling horns—is very effective during the rutting period in early to mid-November. There are some monster bucks living in this region.

I shot this Boone & Crockett Columbia blacktail in northern California, the area that has produced more record-book bucks than any other.

SOUTHERN OREGON

The steep, timbered mountains of southern Oregon are today's "hot spot" for hunting world-class blacktails. The four-county quadrant of Jackson, Douglas, Coos and Josephine counties currently produces the biggest bucks of all, although great bucks come from neighboring counties as well. Here, a combination of spot-and-stalk and stand hunting, sprinkled with calling and rattling during the rut, is the way to go. Want to maximize your chances at a book buck? Apply for one of the region's limited muzzleloader-only tags for a season that runs late into November.

NORTHERN CALIFORNIA

The giant redwood forests of northern California have produced more record-book Columbia blacktails than anywhere else. The area is steep, rugged and heavily timbered, with high-country alpine areas and lots of brush thrown in. Backpacking into remote areas is a good way to go, with the Trinity Alps and Marble Mountains Wilderness Area both excellent choices. Farther south, many private land areas in the San Francisco Bay region are kicking out lots of excellent bucks. Bring good optics and be prepared to glass long and hard.

CENTRAL CALIFORNIA COAST

The official southern boundary for Columbia blacktail runs east/west along the southern borders of Santa Cruz and Santa Clara counties. That said, local deer hunters working San Benito, Monterey and San Luis Obispo counties often erroneously refer to the smallish deer found there as "blacktails," when in truth they are California mule deer. In the '50s and '60s my dad referred to these bucks—which often grew nothing more than forked-horn antlers with very small or no eye guards—as "Pacific bucks." Both these deer and the rugged coastal mountains they inhabit offer a very challenging hunt, and with a general rifle season that opens August 10, be ready for temperatures that can break the century

The World Record Bucks

BOONE & CROCKETT CLUB

Columbia Blacktail: Taken by Lester M. Miller in 1953 in Lewis County, Washington, it scored 182²/₈ points. It was a 4x4 with eye guards, an inside spread of 20²/₈ inches, 5²/₈-inch bases, and a main beam length of 24²/₈ inches (R) and 24⁵/₈ inches (L).

Sitka Blacktail: No one knows who killed this Kodiak Island, Alaska, buck, which scored 128 points. The owner, Craig Allen, bought the antlers from an Anchorage, Alaska, taxidermist. The deer was a 4x4 with eye guards and had a 19⁴/₈-inch inside spread, 4⁷/₈-inch bases, and main beam length of 19⁶/₈ inches (R) and 19 inches (L).

POPE AND YOUNG CLUB

Columbia Blacktail (Typical): Taken by B.J. Shurtleff in 1969 in Marion County, Oregon, this big buck scored 172²/₈ points. It was a 4x4 with extra eye guard points, making it a 7x7, with an inside spread of 20⁴/₈ inches, and main beam length of 26³/₈ inches (R) and 25⁷/₈ inches (L).

Columbia Blacktail (Non-Typical): This monster 8x10 buck scored 194⁴/₈ points, and was taken by James Decker in 1988 in Jackson County, Oregon. It had a 19¹/₈-inch inside spread and main beams measuring 23³/₈ inches (R) and 23⁴/₈ inches (L).

Sitka Blacktail: Taken on Prince of Wales Island, Alaska, in 1987 by Charles Hakari, the 4x4 with eye guards scored 116³/₈ points. It had an inside spread of 13¹/₈ inches and main beams measuring 18⁴/₈ inches (R) and 18²/₈ inches (L).

Glassing California blacktail country.

break the century mark. Lots of hiking and spot-and-stalk hunting is the way to go here.

Late at night, I often think about a buck I called Grandfather, simply because he was so big in both body and antler he must have spawned several generations of deer. I saw him only once as he passed through the giant redwoods in a northern California coastal forest, offering no shot. I hunted him for four years after that—hard—annually finding his tracks and once finding one of his sheds, a massive four-point piece of bone that scored 72 B&C inches all by itself. I never did see him again. He simply disappeared, ghost-like.

Then, in 1997, I drew a limited-entry November muzzleloader permit in Oregon. Guide Doug Gattis of Medford and I hunted our petunias off, passing up several dandy bucks until finally, one drizzly morning, the deer I'd been dreaming of all those years appeared. His typical 4x4 antlers officially score 154¹/₈ Boone and Crockett points, making him one of the largest blacktail bucks killed in recent years.

Sometimes dreams do come true.

SITKA BLACKTAILS

Hunting Sitka blacktails is one of the most enjoyable, highly successful deer hunting experiences in all of North America. With blocky bodies that can exceed 200 pounds, and short, heavy antlers, Sitka bucks are both fun and challenging to hunt.

Like Columbia blacktails, the way you hunt Sitka deer depends on where you're hunting them. Here's a look at their habitat types, and the best ways to find deer in each.

KODIAK ISLAND

This is where the highest Sitka blacktail densities and the biggest bucks can be found. The terrain varies from a rolling high-alpine tundra to steep alder-

With high deer densities and superb trophy quality, Kodiak Island, Alaska, is a great place to hunt Sitka blacktails. Spot-and-stalk hunting is by far the best method to find a good buck here.

choked mountainsides to a rolling coastline. Until late in the season the bigger bucks are found up high, and you have to climb to get them. When winter approaches and the rut kicks in, they tend to move lower, though they rarely reach the beaches. Generally, spot-and-stalk techniques work best, while during the rut—late October to mid-November—calling and rattling draws bucks in close. Good deer hunting is found on neighboring Afognak and Raspberry islands too. Sitka deer also are found on many of the islands in Prince William Sound, though both overall numbers and trophy quality is markedly less.

SOUTHEAST ALASKA

Dominated by the huge Tongass National Forest, southeast Alaska—from Yakutat south to Ketchikan—is a steep, rugged region of old-growth timber laced with small streams, large rivers and lakes of all sizes. There is good deer hunting on the mainland, but the best is found on many of the area's islands, including Prince of Wales and the ABCs—Admiralty, Baranof and Chichagof—where both trophy-quality and deer densities are good. Spot-and-stalk techniques apply early, when the deer are in alpine areas above timberline. As the season grows and the rut kicks in, the deer are found inside the thick old-growth timber. Using doe bleat and grunt calls mixed with judicious rattling inside this thick timber is highly effective. A word of caution, though—brown bears have been known to come readily to deer calls, so be prepared.

The Bear Essentials

Much Sitka deer hunting occurs in areas where there are high brown bear densities. Every fall, a deer hunter or two gets swatted by a bear. On a week's deer hunt in brown bear country, the odds are you're going to see some bears.

To that end, you have to be prepared. Some choose to hunt deer with large caliber rifles, like the .338 Win. Mag. and .375 H&H Mag., knowing these cartridges are much more than they need for deer, but will help get them out of trouble should bears become a problem. Others carry pepper spray canisters. The best protection, however, is awareness. Always be on the lookout for bears. Stay out of alder thickets. Keep a clean camp. Try to pack your deer back to camp the same day you shoot it, and then store the meat at least 100 yards downwind of camp. If you must return to pack meat the next day, approach the carcass carefully, glassing from a distance for bears before moving in.

Brown bears are a fascinating animal, and one of the continent's fastest and most powerful. They're not to be taken lightly. Yet being around them is one of the allures of Sitka blacktail hunting. It just wouldn't be the same without them.

Chapter 6

HUNTING TROPHY BUCKS

There are so many thoughts and feelings that run through my mind the night before opening morning. Each is special in its own way. Sometimes I think I'm too comfortable, tucked away in a small motel room in an even smaller town somewhere east of the Continental Divide. Well before first light I'll drive my truck down a two-track road to the edge of a high rim, then walk for an hour in the dark to my glassing station.

On some outfitted hunts it's almost the same, sleeping in a padded bunk, with a full bathroom a few steps down the hall. This time, though, as the bacon is sizzling and coffee perking, I'll help the guides saddle the horses. Today we're going to ride to the top of a big mesa, and glass the finger ridges that lead up from the alfalfa. There's a big supper and lots of camaraderie before bed, and the anticipation of what's to come is as sweet as honey.

Sometimes my camp is a solitary one. I may be sleeping in my camper, parked down some deserted forest service road, waiting to climb high into the peaks by the light of the moon. Often I backpack into the high country for a few days, drinking from crystal-clear streams, eating freeze-dried food, sleeping on the ground. Before bed I sit outside my tent and look at the sky, wondering where all the stars came from.

But no matter where I'm sleeping, my thoughts rarely vary. I dream about bucks. Big bucks. Bucks with antlers so thick at the bases you can't get your hands around them, tines so long they seem to reach for the sky. Usually there are a few cheaters too, "trash factor" points that add a unique character to the dark, mahogany-stained antlers.

In close to 30 years of mule deer hunting, the thought of a set of big antlers still gives me the willies. To say that they are hard to come by is like saying Astaire could dance, Koufax could bring it, Hitler was a bad guy. An understatement of epic proportions. It takes dedication, planning, research, skill with one's chosen weapon, hard work and more than a little luck to make the dream come true.

The night before opening day is all about hope. Hope that sometime tomorrow your glasses will pick up antlers that will take your breath away, hope that you'll be able to move into position for the shot, hope that the inevitable "buck fever" won't overcome your shooting skills.

Hope that tomorrow is your day of destiny. It just might be ...

FINDING MR. BIG

*I*t was a frigid, snowy November's day, and I was shivering—but not from the cold. The mule deer buck with the oversized antlers slinking through the lodgepole gave me a case of buck fever that I was trying desperately to control. His horns looked as big around as the trees, their tines as long as the pine's main branches. It was a scene I'll never forget.

The deer moved from other hunters who blindly stomped around in the timber below. Later, his tracks showed he circled them. If he continued on course, he'd pass through a 50-yard-wide opening not 100 yards below where I sat on an old rotten stump.

He paused at the opening, radar senses tuned to the world around him. Then he surprised me by not walking, but running, through the clearing. It was all I could do to get my rifle on him and squeeze the trigger. If it had been a 30-yard opening, I never would have gotten my act together in time.

That was the first really exceptional muley buck I ever had a crack at. His heavy, 5x6 antlers later measured 29¹/₂ inches wide, and carried their mass from base to tips. It was also the only time I ever lucked into a trophy-class buck.

That was back in the late 1970s, in Idaho's Adams County, near McCall. It also sowed the seed of trophy mule deer hunting in my blood. After that season I

I took this bruiser buck on a January archery-only hunt in New Mexico as he was tending a herd of does, two of which remained in estrus. It took eight days to fool all those smart does long enough to get a shot at the buck.

made looking for oversized bucks something of a mission. And while I've learned a lot after nearly 20 years in search of large mulies (and still have much more to learn), three lessons stand out.

First, it ain't easy. In fact, in light of all the pressures mule deer populations are under these days, and after spending an inordinate amount of time hunting just about every North American big game species, I think finding trophy-class muley bucks is just about the most difficult task hunters face on the continent today. Second, to be successful on mature, trophy-class mulies on any kind of a regular basis, it's better to be lucky than good. And third, those who work hardest at it are usually the luckiest.

TROPHY BUCKS: WHAT ARE THEY?

Biologists will tell you that any antlered animal needs three things to become a "trophy." First, it must have the genetic makeup to grow eye-popping antlers. Animals without the required genetics simply can't grow a trophy-class set of horns. Second, it must have a

diet rich in protein and certain minerals (like calcium and phosphorus), as well as adequate water, so it can physically reach its full potential. Not all portions of the mule deer's range in North America have the minerals needed to do the job. And third, it must be able to grow old enough to put the first two things to work. Bucks that are killed before they reach their fifth year simply will not produce the largest antlers they can.

Taking this into consideration, I lump trophy bucks into two distinct categories. "Class One" bucks are deer with true record book potential. These animals are as rare as a politician that keeps his promises. Their antlers have the mass, spread and tine length to make casual hunters gawk and serious buck hunters reach for their heart medicine. They are found only in a few select areas of the country. Even when you're in the right place, they're harder to catch than the greased pig at the county fair.

"Class Two" bucks are what I also call "local trophy bucks." These are the oldest, most mature bucks in any given area of the country. While they may not have the genetics, food or soil mineral content to

I define trophy class bucks as the oldest bucks living in a given area, regardless of the size of their antlers. Any muley buck that's lived more than 4 years will be tough to take.

grow eye-popping racks, they have survived through at least four or five years of life, and become just as difficult to find as Class One bucks.

One example of Class Two bucks are the California mule deer (a mule deer subspecies) that inhabit the rugged coastal mountains of the central California coast. I cut my teeth on these deer and have taken several that were over five years of age. The largest antlers are generally only big-forked horns, with perhaps a small third point jutting out from the main beam, and often with no eye guards. A huge antler spread here is 21 inches. (These are the ones my dad used to call "Pacific bucks.") They may not have been bucks for the record book, but a Pacific buck from this country, like my largest—a 23-inch-wide three-pointer—is as hard to find as a near Boone and Crockett qualifying buck from an area with the potential to produce them.

For that reason, hunters without record-book-class

deer in their own back yards, and without the wherewithal to travel and hunt where trophy deer realistically *might* be, can still employ the following hunting tactics as they pursue Class Two bucks. That's my definition of trophy deer hunting—seeking out the oldest, most mature bucks in any given area. No matter their antler size, if they have survived at least four years, they'll have a bag of tricks that would make Houdini green with envy.

HUNTING TROPHY-CLASS BUCKS

We've all read the articles and heard the talk about how dumb mule deer bucks are. The myth is that they run away from hunters, but stop and look back before crossing a ridge, where they make easy pickings for a good rifle shot.

Trophy mule deer are the sneakiest, most coyote-like animals I've ever hunted—and that includes big whitetails. These deer live in the thickest, brushiest, most heavily timbered places in their home range. They know that inaccessible country gives them safety from their most-feared enemy—man. I believe that the older a mule deer buck gets, the smaller his home range becomes. He knows every inch of it like you know your back yard.

Rule number one in hunting big bucks is to hunt areas where human pressure is minimal. A radio tag collar study conducted in Idaho confirmed what many of us have always believed—that once hunting season starts, or human pressure increases dramatically, the older bucks do one of three things: They leave the area for a new home range; move into the most inaccessible canyons, brush piles or rim rock areas of their current home range; or are shot and killed.

"Unpressured" does not necessarily mean 20 miles off the trail head. It can mean a small pocket of overlooked territory next to a road or behind a ranch house. For example, some of the biggest bucks I ever saw were lying in the thick brush on steep hillsides right next to dirt roads used by hundreds of cars every day. In fact, one of the largest bucks I ever saw killed was a giant deer that green-scored 212 Boone and Crockett points, shot in the Kaibab Plateau of Arizona. He was lying on a northeast-facing hillside covered with thick oak brush, bedded for the day in complete safety, as hunter-loaded trucks whizzed by not 200 yards below his bed. I'm sure he'd been bedding on that same hillside for years.

Inexperienced hunters don't give big mule deer bucks the credit they deserve when it comes to their ability to detect human presence. This is probably because the deer are so good at evading a not-too-serious hunter that he never even knows a buck has duped him. Most people know that deer can smell very well, and that their senses of hearing and sight are good too. What they don't understand is that mature bucks fine-tune their senses into a high-tech radar system that detects the slightest change in their familiar environment.

To that end, always check the wind when hunting. I use butane lighters or a small puff bottle filled with powdered carpenter's chalk, and check wind direction several times an hour, and more often when I'm getting close on a stalk. Never talk, bang metal or wear scratchy clothing. They call them mule deer because of their mule-like ears, and these oversized hearing aids really pick up sound in the still mountain air.

A big buck hunting rule: Don't ignore the wind.

by them at a distance of less than 10 feet. I've seen huge bucks bedded in heavy brush lie there as hunters shot at them a dozen times and missed, the bullets hitting less than a foot from them.

Spot-and-stalk hunting is generally the way to go most of the time, though there are times when setting a treestand or ground blind over a water hole, or on a well-scouted trail in heavy timber is dynamite. And on occasion, drives will kick out some decent bucks. But by and large, the best way to hunt truly big bucks is to access the area like a Stealth bomber, slipping in under the deer's radar, staying under that radar screen all day long as you let your eyes do the walking, then slipping out again the same way if you are not successful that day.

Large-antlered muley bucks are as tough to hunt as any deer species on the continent, including whitetails.

When hiking, always assume that the deer are looking for you. Never cross saddles standing upright, and never skyline yourself on ridgetops. Whenever possible, walk in the shade, not the bright sunlight. Remove shiny objects from your gear and clothing that might reflect sunlight.

I've never witnessed a drive that pushed trophy-class mule deer in front of standers. Average bucks, yes. But a deer gets big by hiding, not running. I've literally stepped on them in thick oak brush patches as they were going to let me walk right

An often-overlooked key to hunting big mulies is to find an area that holds large bucks, then hunt it year after year. An intimate knowledge of both the terrain and the deer's habits there are invaluable.

FINAL THOUGHTS

Hunting Class One trophy mule deer bucks isn't something you expect to accomplish in one season. It is the rare hunter who takes a record-class buck ever in his or her lifetime, let alone the first season or two. In reality, it is a lifelong quest in search of a pocket of trophy bucks in an area that, once discovered, may be hunted for several years until the dice finally roll you a "7."

Because I always like to peek over the next ridgeline just to see what's on the other side, I'm constantly hunting new areas. This really isn't conducive to trophy-deer hunting. A better plan is to research several areas, hunt them until you find one that has the kind of deer you're interested in, then go back and hunt that same area year after year. An intimate knowledge of a given area can be your best friend when it comes to understanding exactly where the deer live, how they act and what they'll do when pressured.

No matter how you slice it, hunting trophy mule deer bucks is one of modern hunting's toughest challenges. It also is one of its most rewarding. By systematically researching areas, then hunting them hard and staying with it, your chances of success will increase dramatically.

When Hunting Big Bucks...

- Always keep the wind in your favor, even if you have not yet spotted any deer.
- Always take care with your scent in the hunting area. Try not to "stink up the place" by overhunting a potential big buck hole unless conditions are right to move in and shoot the deer that day.
- Never wear scratchy, noisy clothing. Remove all bright, shiny objects from your clothing and gear. Don't bang truck doors shut, rub metal on metal or snap branches. When walking, be as quiet as possible.

- Always keep talking to a minimum, and when you must speak, whisper.
- Never skyline yourself when walking. Stay in the shadows and other cover. Always assume that a buck is out there someplace, looking for you.
- Become proficient with your weapon of choice and be able to make the shot quickly under tough field conditions. Rare is the hunter who gets more than one opportunity at a giant buck. When yours comes, you must be able to make the shot count.

TODAY'S TOP TROPHY AREAS

*I*f there's one thing I've learned about big game hunting over the years, it's that, no matter how badly you want to, you can't shoot an animal if it isn't there. That statement definitely applies to trophy mule deer bucks.

As previously discussed, mule deer need three things to grow the kinds of antlers that give even seasoned deer hunters the "shakes"—the right genetics; the right nutrition, including soil mineral content; and the chance to grow to at least five years of age, and preferably older.

In most areas of the West, game managers have managed mule deer herds for quantity rather than quality. That is to say, rather than limit the number of bucks harvested from a given area or herd by limiting

the number of tags issued each fall, they instead issue a higher number of tags that results in more bucks harvested each year, making it extremely difficult for a buck to live past his third or fourth birthday. Also, there are few areas of the country that have the nutrition and soil mineral content needed to grow maximum-sized antlers, and even fewer areas that have the genetics in the local deer herd to grow record-class headgear.

Even areas that have the "Big Three" trophy-antler factors in their favor don't produce oversized antlers every year. Climatic cycles, like drought, adversely affect antler growth. So can increased predation, seen more each year in areas where mountain lion and coyote hunting and trapping have been restricted or eliminated. Human encroachment is another over-looked factor. With more subdivisions and small "ranchette"-style houses being built daily on prime winter range and the historic travel corridors mule have used for centuries between summer and winter range, deer numbers and trophy quality suffer.

The bottom line is that, if hunting true trophy-class bucks is your passion, you need to stay on top of what's happening in the areas you hunt on an annual basis. Things change. Yesterday's trophy hot spot can be void of big bucks tomorrow. An area that produced big bucks in the 1960s but hasn't been known for them in 20 years can suddenly start kicking out a few good ones again. Serious trophy hunters do everything they can to stay on the leading edge of the curve, where the big buck potential is on the rise, rather than the trailing edge, where a once shining light is fading.

TROPHY BUCK HUNTING *TODAY*

Knowing that things can change suddenly, I turned to Garth Carter of Garth Carter's Hunter's Services (P.O. Box 45, Minersville, UT 84752; (435)386-1020,

www.huntinfool.com on the World Wide Web) for help in finding today's top trophy mule deer areas. Carter, an ex-biologist for the state of Utah, is a serious trophy hunter, with mule deer as one of his passions. His business is researching the best trophy areas and passing the information on to his clients. Here's what he has to say:

"A lot of states are going to giving out some form of 'guaranteed' tags," Carter says. "That can be 'X' number of tags guaranteed each year to a certain guide or outfitter, a landowner and so on. Buying one of these tags is the best way to ensure that you will be able to hunt the best areas during the best seasons, if you're willing to go guided. That's one way to beat the system."

"However, there are still some excellent hunts on public land yielding some dandy bucks for the hunter who is willing to pay his dues by researching, scouting and hunting hard," Carter says. "The limited-entry tags are gold in the right areas, if you can draw them.

"Generally speaking, in the Rocky Mountain states like Utah, Colorado, southern Idaho, Montana, and Wyoming, as well as northern Arizona and New

Mexico, you should look for hunts on or after November 1, so you are getting at least the beginning of the rut," Carter advises. "Look for high-desert units, at the 4,000- to 6,000-foot elevation, that have high pinion and juniper cover. This type of cover makes it virtually impossible to kill the mature bucks, who rarely expose themselves during daylight hours. But during the rut, they come out into the more open sagebrush flats, where the does are, and then become somewhat vulnerable." The rut timing varies, of course, with the rut occurring earlier in November in the northern tier of the U.S. and southern British Columbia, Alberta and Saskatchewan, and in late December and early January in southern Arizona, New Mexico and Sonora, Mexico.

Carter also stresses that trophy hunters not overlook any archery-only and muzzle-loader-only hunts in these states, because they produce super hunting and a chance at some really big bucks.

Here's Carter's assessment of the best trophy-hunting potential in the most popular mule deer states:

Bucks like this bruiser don't grow on trees. To find one, you have to hunt those few areas in the West that consistently produce such eye-popping racks.

ALASKA

Kodiak Island has the best Sitka blacktail hunting in the world, in terms of both deer numbers and big bucks. Keep on top of how the winters have hit Kodiak as you plan any hunt. Particularly harsh snowfalls and cold will kill a lot of deer and hunting will suffer in the following couple of seasons. The same is true on massive Prince of Wales Island in southeast Alaska, another area where deer numbers are high and trophy potential is good.

Barrow

Nome

NORTON SOUND

Yukon River

Fairbanks

Tok

Kuskokwim River

Anchorage

Juneau

GULF OF ALASKA

Kodiak Island

Prince of Wales Island

BRISTOL BAY

ARIZONA

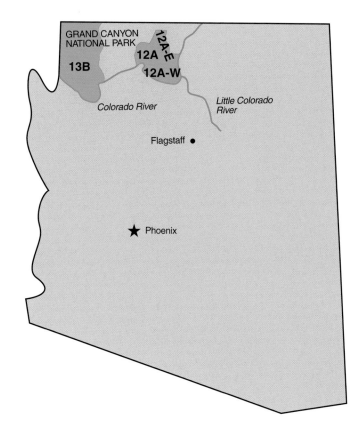

All units north of the Colorado River, including the Kaibab Plateau and Arizona Strip, have big buck potential. The Kaibab is coming back but is a very weather-dependent unit. That is, following years of severe drought you have a lower overall deer population because of lower fawn recruitment. But three to four years of good moisture in a row means that three to four years after that is the time to hunt because there will be good numbers of mature bucks available.

Arizona's top mule deer units: 12A E, 12A W (late), 12A E (muzzleloader), 13B (Carter's choice as the best rifle hunt in the state).

COLORADO

The state's northwest corner is seeing a real comeback in the number of good bucks seen each year. Also, the state's eastern plains from the northeast to southeast has relatively low mule deer densities but some dandy bucks. It typically takes one to five years to draw, and most of the better hunting is on private land. "The December 1 through 15 hunt is the one to hunt here; the rut is on and it can be dynamite, $^7/_8$" Carter says.

Carter's choices for the very best Colorado trophy mule deer rifle hunting

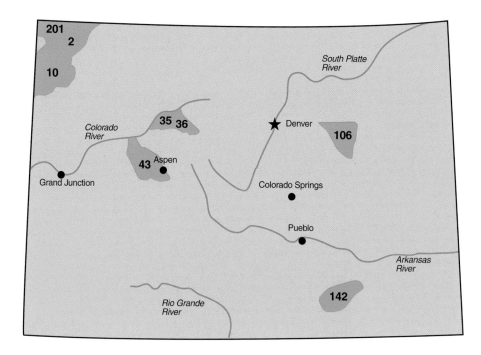

include hunting in units 2, 10, 35, 36, 43, 106 and 142. Muzzleloaders may want to try their hand in units 2, 10, 43 and 201, while bowhunters should try the early archery season in units 2, 10 and 201.

IDAHO

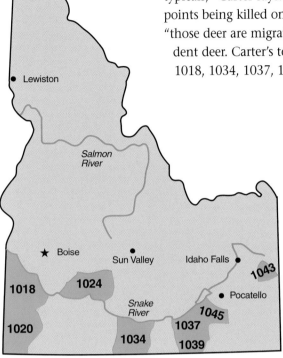

Generally speaking, the southern half of the state and its handful of November rifle buck tags can be "really good tags for some huge non-typicals," Carter says. "There are bucks scoring over 230 Boone and Crockett points being killed on these hunts from time to time." According to Carter, "those deer are migrating to the winter range during the rut, and are not resident deer. Carter's top Idaho units for rifle hunters include 1024, 1020, 1018, 1034, 1037, 1039, 1043 and 1045.

MONTANA

This is the only state left where you can hunt mule deer during the rut on a general deer license. The result is that in many areas, particularly west of the Continental Divide, the deer have been hammered, buck-to-doe ratios are very low and trophy bucks are extremely rare. Montana's best mule deer hunting occurs in the state's southeastern quadrant, in Region 7, primarily because the best mule deer habitat is found on private land and the landowners conduct

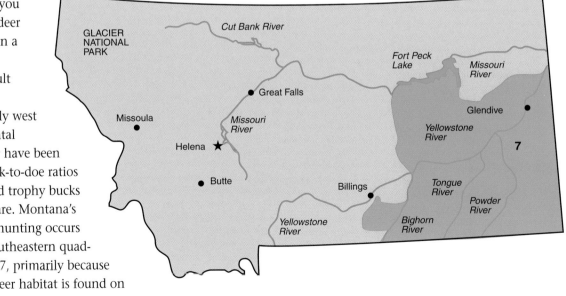

their own management programs by limiting hunter access. In Montana, finding a buck that scores more than 185 Boone and Crockett points is rare today.

The entire state is very good for mule deer hunting because that state has forced everyone, including residents, to draw for every available mule deer tag. "Really, just about every unit has the potential to produce a book typical and giant non-typical trophy muley," says Carter. His picks for the state's very best rifle hunts include units 014, 015, 021, 033 and 111-115 (late).

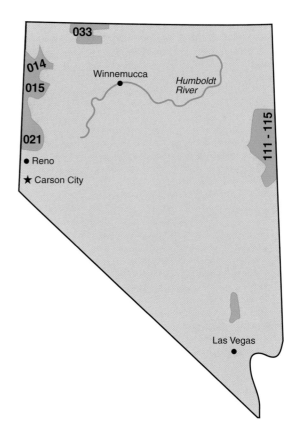

NEW MEXICO

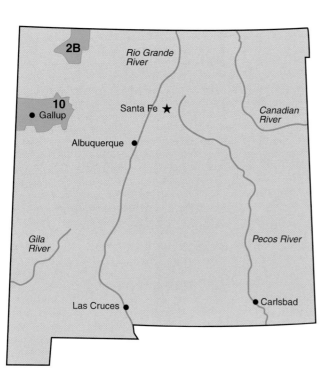

Carter calls New Mexico a "poor choice for the true trophy mule deer hunter. There are plenty of deer, but the trophy potential is low. A few big bucks come from the state, but they are rare." He recommends Subunit 2B and Zuni Unit 10 as the two top big-buck areas of the state.

Carter calls Oregon "the real sleeper state for trophy mule deer hunting." Why? Because the state offers no rifle rut hunts, and the deer are so scattered they're not getting concentrated hunting pressure. "The eastern half of the state is very good, and can produce some fantastic bucks," Carter says. The best units for big mulies include the Beulah, Malheur River, Juniper, Steens Mountain and Trout Creek units, as well as Lookout Mountain. Hart Mountain and North Warner also have trophy muley potential.

Oregon is also the top state right now for trophy Columbia blacktails. The state's late-season muzzleloader-only limited-entry hunts are, by far, the best chance found throughout the blacktail's range to take a Boone and Crockett buck on public land. Apply for the Applegate (128M) and N Muzzleloader (100M1) units. Generally speaking, the biggest blacktails come from the four counties found in the state's southwest corner.

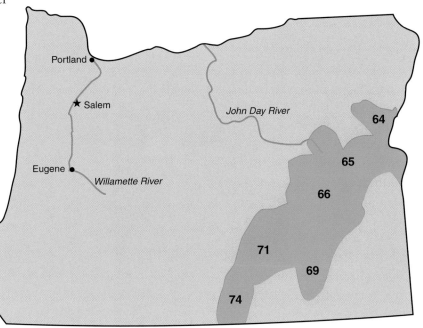

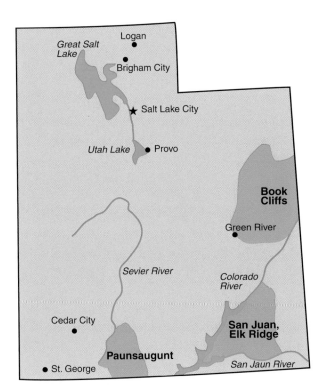

Utah is one of those states that has excellent genetics but has been managed for maximum hunter opportunity rather than quality. Hence, finding trophy-class bucks in Utah is tough. The best chances occur on private ranches, and those tags cost an arm and a leg. The Book Cliffs area is one exception, with plenty of public but remote country that can grow big bucks. The other well-known trophy buck units in Utah are in the southern part of the state. They are San Juan Elk Ridge and Paunsaugunt. "These traditional areas are still very good, but not as good as they once were," Carter says. "The age class is down due to the numbers of permits issued, but the genetics are there." Carter also likes the Dolores Triangle area, where his wife killed a 199 B&C buck a few years back.

"It is not as good a mule deer state as it has been in the past, nor are they coming back all that quickly," Carter admits. "However, the state does produce some real dandies every year. You just have to hunt long and hard to find them." Regions G & H, in the high country and during the early September hunts, can be good, but you need to be a strong backpacker or have horses to hunt them effectively, Carter suggests. Some November 1 through 15 rifle hunts are available on a limited basis, and good deer are taken during these hunts too, Carter says. Look into hunts in units 120, 125, 128 and 129. In

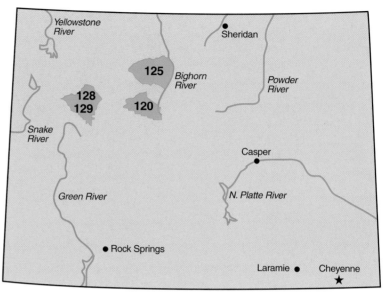

Region C virtually all the land is private, and you need to secure trespass rights before applying.

"OTHER" TROPHY MULEY AREAS

Big bucks are, as they say, where you find them. To that end, some areas that you might not think of as producing trophy mulies are doing just that these days.

In Canada, southeastern British Columbia and southern Alberta have been producing a few dandy bucks in recent years. However, nonresident aliens—Americans—are required to hire a licensed guide to hunt them. If you're interested, contact a reputable booking agent for more information.

Places like western Kansas and western Texas have been producing some great mulies in recent years. However, hunting opportunity for nonresidents is very limited. But researching these states just might open your eyes to a potential trophy mule deer hunt you just can't resist.

I've hunted Sonora, Mexico, several times for mule deer, and I've taken my two best bucks from there. One is a heavy, typical-framed 6x7 with a 37-inch outside spread. The other is a non-typical with 34^1/$_2$-inch outside spread, 16 scorable points and scores 243 Boone and Crockett points despite having his left G-2 and right eye guard broken off. They are both true monster bucks.

However, Sonora is an all-or-nothing hunt. I didn't kill my first big buck until the last afternoon of the

"Alternative" Weapons & Big Bucks

Most mule deer hunters are rifle hunters. They love their pet deer rifles, and would never consider hunting mulies without them. And yet, in so doing they are severely restricting their chances at hunting true trophy-class bucks. That's because many states are setting aside limited-entry areas for hunting many different western big game species—including mule deer—in which you are only allowed to hunt with a more "primitive" weapon, specifically, a muzzleloader or archery tackle.

Limited-entry, or special-draw, hunts are becoming more and more common each year throughout the West for many species of big game, but especially mule deer and elk. You can find more specific information about these hunts and how to apply for them in the next section of this chapter, "How to Draw the Best in the West." The more you look into these hunts, the more you realize that you have a much broader selection of hunts to choose from, with

In many cases, the best trophy muley hunts are restricted to the use of archery tackle or muzzleloaders. Switching from the centerfire rifle to one of these weapons is a great way to increase your odds for a trophy-class buck.

many of those hunts set during the rut, if you choose a weapon other than your centerfire rifle. What this means is that if you can draw one of these tags, you can hunt mature bucks in areas that have historically produced better-than-average bucks with less competition from other hunters than you find almost anywhere on public land during the general deer season.

I got back into bowhunting in a big way many years ago when states began severely restricting and/or eliminating hunting rutting elk with a rifle, but expanded bugle hunts for archers. Today I love to bowhunt, and find

some excellent mule deer hunts for archers only. At the same time, more and more rut hunts for mulies are popping up each year for muzzleloader hunters. So I began shooting in-line muzzleloaders a few years ago, which produced one Boone and Crockett Columbia black-tail for me in 1997. A picture of this buck appears on page 47.

You raise the odds of putting yourself in the same type of picture next season by leaving the rifle at home and applying for a limited-entry hunt restricted to primitive weapons.

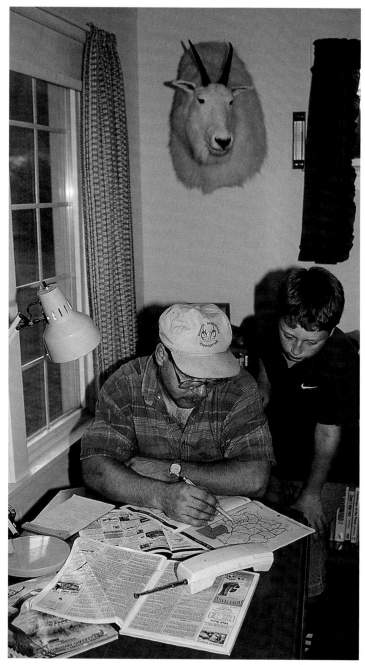

last day of my third hunt. I shot a good buck on my second trip, a 3x4 with 29½-inch spread, but never chambered a round on my first hunt. Why did I keep going back again and again if I had so little success? Because I saw a couple of other true monster bucks taken by other clients, and just knew if I put my time in and got a little bit lucky, sooner or later my day would come. And it has. Twice.

The keys to a successful Sonora hunt are going with the right outfitter at the right time. The right time is in January, when the deer are rutting. While there are several outfitters offering Sonora hunts, I personally know two whose ethics and reputations are above reproach. Alex Ramoz (1245 Fleming Avenue, San Jose, CA 95127; (408)251-2087) is the man with whom I have booked all my Sonora mule deer adventures. He's always treated me right. Jim Schaafsma of Arrow Five Outfitters (Star Rt. 1, Box 64A, Zenia, CA 95595; (707)923-9633) has been outfitting in both Sonora and the West for a variety of big game for many years, and is solid as a rock. Both will give you your money's worth.

ARE YOU A *REAL* TROPHY HUNTER?

Trophy mule deer and blacktail hunters are a breed apart. They live, breathe and sleep big bucks. They spend a fair amount of time and money scouting during the off-season. They run up impressive long-distance bills talking deer hunting, both with other fanatics, and with anyone and everyone they think might give them a lead to a new trophy hot spot. They've got the fever, and they know there is no cure. More than anything else, they are a dedicated, focused bunch.

I know the feeling well. Do you?

Trophy muley and blacktail hunters are a breed apart. They live, breathe and eat trophy buck hunting 365 days a year. Are you willing to make this kind of commitment to success?

How to Draw the
Best in the West

very year the competition for mule deer becomes more intense on public lands. And unfortunately, the days of knocking on a rancher's door and getting permission to go deer hunting are rapidly ending. Today, more ranchers are either posting "No Hunting" signs or leasing their hunting rights to outfitters or small groups of well-healed businessmen. The result is that the unattached hunter often finds himself hunting public land areas that are full of other hunters. The end result is that trophy quality in many areas is going down, along with success rates. And the chances of experiencing what many of us deem a quality hunting experience—good numbers of animals, pristine country and low hunter pressure—is becoming harder to come by.

That's why you should always apply for special-draw hunts.

What Are Special-Draw Hunts?

Virtually every state in the West offers several special hunts, in which mule deer tag numbers are reduced, their issuance tightly controlled and the deer managed for relatively high buck-to-doe ratios. Often, but not always, these hunts restrict hunters to the harvest of only old, mature bucks. In many cases, special-draw hunts place weapons restrictions on hunters, limiting them to using a muzzleloader or archery tackle. And like just about every too-good-to-be-true deal in this world, it pays to read the fine print. In the case of the best special hunts, competition for available tags is fierce. For example, the odds of drawing a tag in most of the areas I apply for each year are no better than five to one, and usually much worse.

These difficult odds keep many people from applying. That's fine with me, but I still don't understand their thinking. Applying for these tags is a no-lose situation.

Where to start? Call state and provincial game departments and get their big game hunt booklets and applications.

HOW TO APPLY FOR SPECIAL-DRAW HUNTS

The process begins in winter by contacting the game department of the state(s) you're thinking about hunting. (You can find both their mailing and World Wide Web site addresses later in this book.) Ask for their upcoming year's hunting regulations, special-draw hunt application forms, and any booklets required to apply for the special hunts. Don't dawdle. Applications for some states are due as early as February 1. Fill them out and get them in on time with exactly the required amount of money. If you draw, you receive the license and tag in the mail, and away you go. If you don't draw, the state refunds all application fees, except for a small processing fee.

In some cases, those who apply and do not draw a tag are given a "preference point" by the state. Preference points give preferential treatment in the drawings to those hunters who have applied for a certain type of hunt in previous years and not drawn a tag. In some cases you actually have to apply for several years before you're really in the game, because more people with the maximum allowable number of preference points are in the draw each year than there are tags available.

"I still believe you can kill the best mule deer buck in the world on the right special-draw hunt, as good as you can find on many of the super-expensive private ranch hunts," asserts Garth Carter, president of Garth Carter's Hunter Services. Carter, a former Utah state game biologist, provides prospective western hunters with all the research information they need to apply for the best special-draw hunts in all western states, tips on how to fill out the applications and a member's referral service so you can talk to others about specific trophy areas and how to hunt them.

"I can't believe there are folks who still do not apply for these hunts," Carter says. "After all, if you draw, you're off on a great hunt. If you don't draw, you get your money back and can go ahead and hunt where you normally would anyway. And in many cases you'll be building preference points that will help you draw in subsequent years. It's a no-brainer."

Another similar service is the United States Outfitters Professional Licensing Service, (800) 845-9929. George Taulman's program is inexpensive, and it's a great way for a "regular guy" to keep up with what's happening with both special tag draws and state-by-state hunting prospects. This service lets you get in on the game and apply for some of the great special-draw hunts I've described—and you won't have to spend hours doing the necessary research if you don't want to.

The odds are long on drawing some of the more coveted permits. But someone has to draw, and it might as well be you. However, you can't draw the tag if you don't play the game. For those serious about mule deer hunting, and who want to have a chance at a real wall hanger buck for the least amount of money, the West's special-draw hunts are where it's at.

THE SPREAD MYTH

Big game hunters, like sports world statisticians, like to categorize the objects of their fascination into neat, easy-to-reference numbered packages. The better the "numbers," the more valued the player or animal. For example, at first glance a quarterback with a rating of 99.6 is more effective than one with a rating of 79.6. A point guard that scores 18 points and averages 8 assists a game is more valuable than one who scores 14 points a game and dishes off 6 assists a night. A shortstop that hits .300 is a superstar, a much better player than one who bats just .250.

As all serious sports fans know, none of the above generalizations are necessarily true. The lower-rated quarterback might be leading a team with a strong running game that goes 12–4, while the higher rated quarterback may only be able to produce an 8–8 record. The high-scoring basketball player may be a pigeon on defense, while his counterpart makes the all-league defensive team and rebounds like a demon. The hard-hitting shortstop just might lead the league in errors at his position, while the other guy might be a Golden Glove winner. When you look at the big picture, which player would you rather have on your team?

The same is true when evaluating antlered big game animal trophy potential. For example, for most mule deer hunters the Holy Grail is a 30-incher—an animal with an antler spread of at least 30 inches. Hunters who travel to the north country to hunt the great Alaska-Yukon moose hope to find an animal with at least a 70-inch inside spread. Optimistic hunters of the Columbian black-tailed deer often talk about finding a buck with a 24-inch spread. Even whitetail hunters have gotten into the act in recent years. When I ask hunters I meet around the country each season how they did, they often answer excitedly, "I got a 22-inch 10-pointer this year!"

All animals that meet the above spread numbers are certainly tremendous trophies. But if you seek an animal that meets hunting's toughest record book minimum—that set by the Boone and Crockett Club—antler spread is a most deceiving number. Just as when

comparing the relative value of athletes, one must look at the total package before making judgments about an animal's honest record-book potential.

To prove the point, I used the 10th edition of the Boone and Crockett Club's *Records of North American Big Game* book as a reference. The 10th edition—hereafter referred to as "the book"—does not feature some of the most recent and exciting new record entries. But for

An antler spread of 30 inches is the Holy Grail of mule deer hunting, yet bucks with these wide spreads rarely make the record book. My Sonoran 37-incher barely would.

our purposes—a comparison of antler spread versus record-book potential—it gives all the data we need.

The 30-Inch Mule Deer

When it comes to quickly equating a spread number with trophy quality, nowhere is it more prevalent than with the mule deer. For decades, the 30-inch muley has been the magic number that revs a hunter's hearts into high gear. However, careful study of the book shows you that a 30-inch spread isn't necessarily all it's cracked up to be.

The book contains a total of 450 mule deer that meet the minimum score of 195 points. Of that number, only 15 bucks had an inside spread of 30 inches or more. That's just 3.3 percent! These bucks include the current world record killed by Doug Burris in Dolores County, Colorado, in 1972 that scored 226 4/8 points, and had an inside spread of 30 7/8 inches. Paul Muehlbauer's Number 5 buck, taken in 1967 at Gypsum Creek, Colorado, had a score of 214 3/8 and a spread of 31 3/8 inches. Robert Parke's Number 11 buck, taken in Teton County, Wyoming, in 1967, scored 211 6/8. A pick-up buck owned by John

Scoresheets courtesy and copyright of Boone and Crockett Club®.

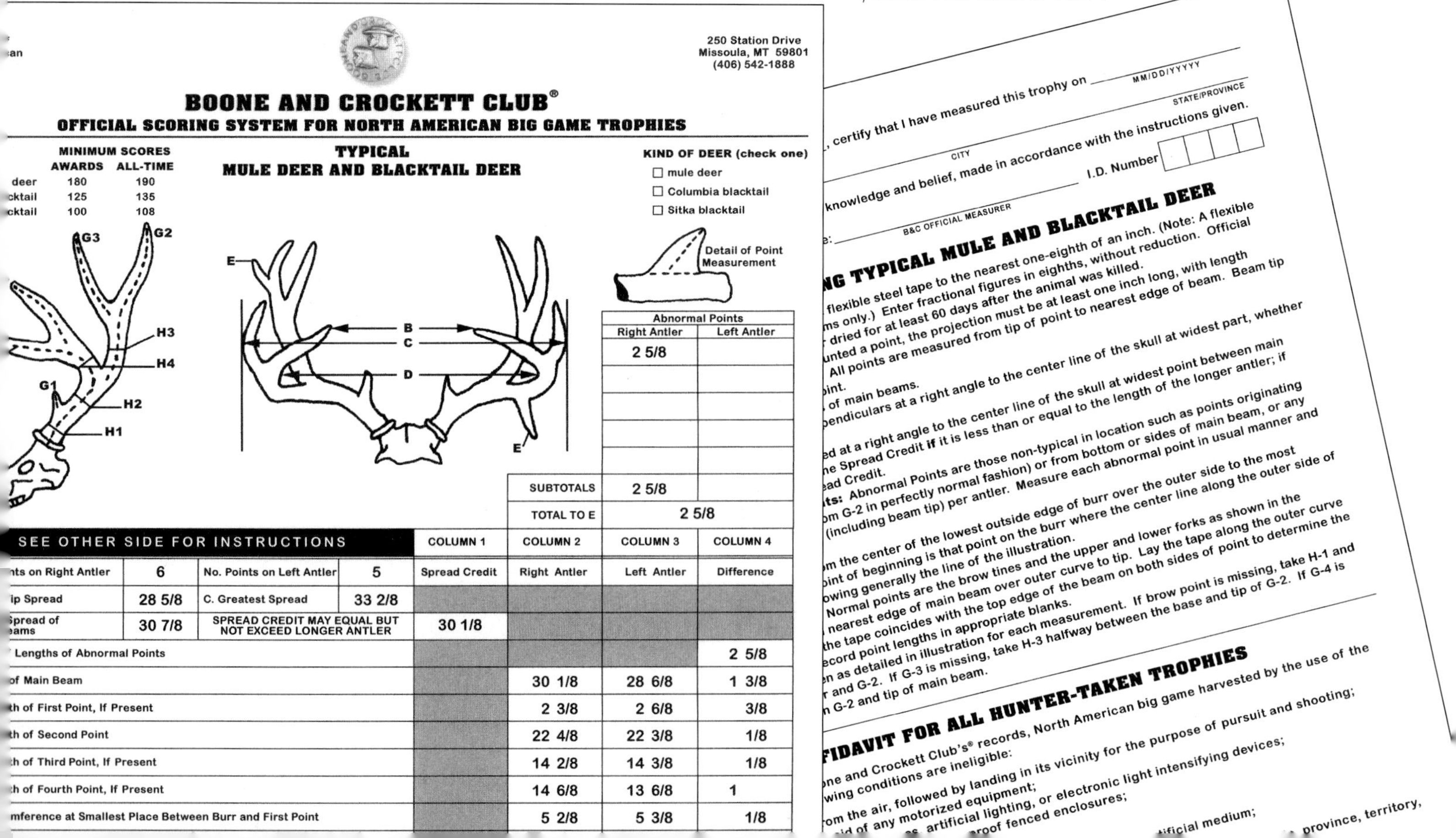

250 Station Drive
Missoula, MT 59801
(406) 542-1888

BOONE AND CROCKETT CLUB®
OFFICIAL SCORING SYSTEM FOR NORTH AMERICAN BIG GAME TROPHIES

MINIMUM SCORES	AWARDS	ALL-TIME
deer	180	190
cktail	125	135
cktail	100	108

TYPICAL MULE DEER AND BLACKTAIL DEER

KIND OF DEER (check one)
☐ mule deer
☐ Columbia blacktail
☐ Sitka blacktail

Abnormal Points Right Antler	Left Antler
2 5/8	
SUBTOTALS 2 5/8	
TOTAL TO E 2 5/8	

SEE OTHER SIDE FOR INSTRUCTIONS				COLUMN 1	COLUMN 2	COLUMN 3	COLUMN 4
nts on Right Antler	6	No. Points on Left Antler	5	Spread Credit	Right Antler	Left Antler	Difference
ip Spread	28 5/8	C. Greatest Spread	33 2/8				
Spread of ams	30 7/8	SPREAD CREDIT MAY EQUAL BUT NOT EXCEED LONGER ANTLER		30 1/8			
Lengths of Abnormal Points							2 5/8
of Main Beam					30 1/8	28 6/8	1 3/8
th of First Point, If Present					2 3/8	2 6/8	3/8
th of Second Point					22 4/8	22 3/8	1/8
h of Third Point, If Present					14 2/8	14 3/8	1/8
h of Fourth Point, If Present					14 6/8	13 6/8	1
mference at Smallest Place Between Burr and First Point					5 2/8	5 3/8	1/8

, certify that I have measured this trophy on ________ MM/DD/YYYY
CITY ________ STATE/PROVINCE
knowledge and belief, made in accordance with the instructions given.
B&C OFFICIAL MEASURER ________ I.D. Number

NG TYPICAL MULE AND BLACKTAIL DEER

flexible steel tape to the nearest one-eighth of an inch. (Note: A flexible ms only.) Enter fractional figures in eighths, without reduction. Official dried for at least 60 days after the animal was killed.
unted a point, the projection must be at least one inch long, with length All points are measured from tip of point to nearest edge of beam. Beam tip oint.
of main beams.
pendiculars at a right angle to the center line of the skull at widest part, whether
d at a right angle to the center line of the skull at widest point between main e Spread Credit if it is less than or equal to the length of the longer antler; if ad Credit.
ts: Abnormal Points are those non-typical in location such as points originating om G-2 in perfectly normal fashion) or from bottom or sides of main beam, or any (including beam tip) per antler. Measure each abnormal point in usual manner and
m the center of the lowest outside edge of burr over the outer side to the most oint of beginning is that point on the burr where the center line along the outer side of owing generally the line of the illustration.
Normal points are the brow tines and the upper and lower forks as shown in the nearest edge of main beam over outer curve to tip. Lay the tape along the outer curve the tape coincides with the top edge of the beam on both sides of point to determine the ecord point lengths in appropriate blanks.
n as detailed in illustration for each measurement. If brow point is missing, take H-1 and r and G-2. If G-3 is missing, take H-3 halfway between the base and tip of G-2. If G-4 is n G-2 and tip of main beam.

FIDAVIT FOR ALL HUNTER-TAKEN TROPHIES

ne and Crockett Club's® records, North American big game harvested by the use of the wing conditions are ineligible:
om the air, followed by landing in its vicinity for the purpose of pursuit and shooting;
id of any motorized equipment;
artificial lighting, or electronic light intensifying devices;
roof fenced enclosures;
tificial medium;
province, territory,

McClendon, entered in 1985, came from Cococino County, Arizona, and scored 209$^5/_8$ to put it in a tie for Number 15; it had a spread of 30$^7/_8$ inches. Those are the only 30-inchers in the top 25.

The widest buck in the book is David Collis's 35-incher that came from Sonora, Mexico, in 1986. It scored 204$^3/_8$, placing it in a tie for 63rd place.

At the other end of the mule deer spectrum are those bucks that make the book with an inside spread of less than 20 inches. Is this possible? The 10th edition lists nine such bucks, the highest scoring is a deer killed by George Shearer in 1952 in Garfield County, Colorado, that scored an incredible 208$^6/_8$ points, despite having an antler spread of only 17$^4/_8$ inches. It ranks Number 23. The other under-20-inch bucks rank Numbers 62, 93, 172 (two tied), 228, 245, 281 and 346.

Mule deer bucks with a spread of between 27 and 29$^7/_8$ inches account for 84 of the 450 10th edition bucks, or 18.7 percent. The largest group of record-book bucks had an inside antler spread of between just 24 and 26$^7/_8$ inches—217 total entries, or 48.2 percent of the total listed. The second-largest group had an inside spread of between 20 and 23$^7/_8$ inches—125 entries, or 27.8 percent of the total listed. One of these bucks, taken in 1962 by Charles Bentley near Grand Junction, Colorado, had an inside spread of 20$^5/_8$ inches and scored 204$^3/_8$ points—tying it for 63rd place with Dave Collis's 35-incher!

TINE LENGTH, MASS, SYMMETRY SCORE HIGH

With mule deer and their close cousins, the blacktails, the key components of record-book score are the length of the main beam and the antler tines, antler mass and symmetry. According to Boone and Crockett scoring rules, inside spread is added to the total score *only if it is less than or equal to the length of the longest main beam.* If the spread is wider than the main beam, the main beam length is used as the spread measurement instead. This, in essence, penalizes most wide bucks instead of rewarding them for what they have.

This lesson was driven home to me twice in recent years. The 37-inch-wide muley I took in Sonora, Mexico, had a main beam length of 25 inches, which cost the buck 10 B&C points. On the other hand, an archery buck I took in New Mexico had an inside

Bucks with extra "trash" points may have too many deductions to make the typical record book, and not enough inches to make it as a non-typical, but who cares? This buck may be one of those "tweeners," but he is one hell of a trophy in the record book that matters most—yours.

spread of less than 25 inches, yet scored 183 B&C points, thanks to long tines and good mass. Both bucks score near to each other, yet if they were standing side by side, there's no question which one I'd take. The "Monster from Mexico" would get it every time.

NON-TYPICAL MULE DEER

Non-typical deer are scored differently than typical bucks in that all their antler points are scored. To be counted as a point, the projection must be at least one inch long, with the length exceeding width at one inch or more of length. The antler spread is measured between perpendiculars at a right angle to the center

It takes a whale of a non-typical muley to make the Boone & Crockett Club's minimum score of 240 points. A great non-typical rarely has a spread exceeding 30 inches.

line of the skull at the widest point of the main beams. Again, however, antler spread cannot exceed the length of the longest main beam; if it does, the main beam length is used instead.

There are a total of 364 entries in the 10th edition's non-typical mule deer category that exceed the minimum score of 240 points. Of that Number, just 17 bucks, or 4.7 percent, exceed 30 inches in inside spread. The largest is the Number 3 buck, taken by William Murphy in 1943 on Arizona's Kaibab Plateau. It scored 324 1/8 points, had a spread of 32 7/8 inches and a total of 43 scorable points. Only two other bucks with a 30-inch spread cracked the top 25. They were Bradley Barclay's 1971 Malheur County, Oregon, buck that scored 297 7/8 and ranks 17; and Albert Mulnix's 1928 Eagle County, Colorado, buck that scored 286 7/8, and ranks Number 23.

The most amazing of all the non-typical book bucks is the current Number 2, taken by Alton Hunsaker in 1943 in Box Elder County, Utah. It scored 330 1/8 points, yet had an inside spread of just 9 4/8

inches! It had 21 scorable points on the right antler, and 28 on the left. Two other book bucks had inside spreads of less than 15 inches. They are the Number 187 deer, taken by Bob Scriver in 1934 in Glacier County, Montana, that scored 252 2/8 points, had a spread of 14 5/8 inches, and a total of 31 scorable points; and the Number 330 buck, Buzz Faro's 1963 Sanders County, Montana, monster that scored 241 7/8 with an inside spread of 14 7/8 inches and 27 scorable points.

In the non-typical category, 143 deer had inside spreads of between 25 and 29 7/8 inches (39.3 percent), while 170 had spreads between 20 and 24 7/8 inches (46.7 percent). Thirty-one bucks, or 8.5 percent, had inside spreads between 15 and 19 7/8 inches.

COLUMBIAN BLACK-TAILED DEER

I've always had a soft spot in my heart for blacktails, having grown up hunting them in California's rugged coastal mountains and forests. These deer are vastly underrated in terms of the difficulty required to harvest a record-class deer. I truly believe a true fair-chase book blacktail is the most difficult of all our deer species to come by, along with a book mule deer.

Blacktail hunters like to talk about bucks with a two-foot spread. And yet, of the 603 typical blacktails listed in the book that exceed the minimum score of 130 points, just 10 (1.7 percent) have spreads of at least 24 inches. The highest scoring is the Number 8 buck, which scored 166 2/8 points and had a 26⅝-inch spread. It was taken in Glenn County, California, by Peter Gerbo in 1949. The other 24-inch-plus book bucks rank Number 21, 23, 29, 40, 47, 60 and 97. The largest spread in the book is the Number 60 buck, taken in Trinity County, California, in 1930 by A.H. Hilbert. It had a spread of 28 6/8 inches.

A total of 118 book blacktails have a spread of between 20 and 23 7/8 inches (19.6 percent). These include Lester Miller's world-record buck, a monster scoring 182 2/8 points with a spread of 20 2/8 inches. It was taken in Lewis County, Washington, in 1953. The Number 2 buck had a spread of 21 4/8 inches, scored 170 6/8 points, and was taken by Clark Griffith in 1962 near Elk City, Oregon. The Number 4 blacktail scored 170 points, had a spread of 20 2/8 inches, and was taken in 1989 by Wayne Despain in Jackson County, Oregon.

The most book blacktails have an inside spread between 16 and 19 7/8 inches—a total of 362, or 60

A great blacktail buck in velvet.

percent. The Number 3 buck scored $170^{1}/_{8}$ points, had a spread of $19^{5}/_{8}$ inches, and was taken in 1963 by Woodrow Gibbs in Linn County, Oregon. Bucks in this spread category also account for the Number 5, 6, 7, 12, 13, 16, 17, 18, 19, 21, 24, 26, 29 and 31 bucks.

Interestingly, a total of 113 book bucks, or 18.7 percent, have inside spreads of between just 12 and $15^{7}/_{8}$ inches. The largest is the Number 28 buck, which had a spread of $14^{7}/_{8}$ inches, scored $159^{4}/_{8}$ points, and was taken by Russ McClennan in Mendocino County, California, in 1984. The smallest inside spread found in the book is the Number 584 buck, taken by Michael Demery in Cowlitz County, Washington, in 1978. It scored $130^{4}/_{8}$ points, and had a spread of just $12^{4}/_{8}$ inches.

As is the case with their mule deer cousins, main beam length, antler tine length, antler mass and symmetry are the key factors in making "the book."

Defining Trophy Bucks

Record books, such as those compiled by the Boone and Crockett and Pope and Young Clubs, and Safari Club International, are fun to read. The animals entered in these books are spectacular trophies, freaks of nature that grew much larger sets of antlers than the vast majority of their brethren.

However, even if a buck doesn't make "the book," that doesn't mean he isn't a trophy. Mule deer hunters for years have talked about huge bucks with lots of extra points that, when the deer is scored according to official record book criteria, don't count, or have deductions that take away from the deer's official score. Mike Eastman, a video maker and publisher of Eastman's Journal, a trophy hunter's magazine, coined the term "trash factor" when discussing all the extra points these bucks have that don't officially count in their final "book score." Does this make them unworthy of trophy status? Of course not. In fact, many of us actually love trash-factor bucks above all others. These old, heavily antlered deer have character, and are true trophy bucks despite not scoring high enough on an "official" score sheet.

And besides, what is a trophy mule deer or blacktail buck to one person may not be a trophy buck to someone else. A trophy is often not measured in inches of antler, but in sweat equity or the specialness of a particular hunt. A person's first buck is certainly a trophy to be treasured for a lifetime. Taking your son or daughter out and helping them take their first mule deer—even if it is a doe—is a trophy hunt to be savored forever. A buck killed on a particularly tough hunt might be a real trophy to you, even if it has relatively small antlers.

A "book buck." We'd all like to have one someday. But just because your next muley doesn't quite meet a record club's criteria for entry into their record book, don't feel like you have been unsuccessful. In my mind, and in the minds of many other serious mule deer hunters everywhere, any muley or blacktail buck—or doe, if you're fortunate enough to draw such a tag—you choose to take, when harvested under the rules of fair chase, is a trophy to be proud of.

After all, the only hunter you really need to please is yourself.

This buck has it all—good mass, long beams and tines, lots of "trash" points, and a wide spread. He may not make the book, but so what? He's a dream buck in my book!

Chapter 7

PLANNING YOUR HUNT

Do you like to live life on the edge? Are you the kind of person who lives from paycheck to paycheck? A "life's short, eat dessert first" kind of guy or gal?

If you are, when it comes to your big game hunting success, you're probably the kind of person who assumes that your luck will hold, and you'll be successful without a lot of fuss and muss. The kind who will randomly choose an area to hunt and simply decide to go hunting where someone told you he once shot a good buck, or spend a good chunk of hard-earned money to hire an outfitter you read about someplace. Then you'll just show up the night before opening day, expecting that the deer, knowing you're there, will run out with their little hooves in the air in surrender.

I love people like that. Why? Because they are no threat to my success. While such a strategy might work hunting an eastern whitetail area that's loaded with deer and where the goal is just to put a deer in the freezer, in mule deer country it's a sure formula for disaster. These are the people who help ensure that overall mule deer hunting success rates remain low throughout the animal's range. They leave more good bucks out there for me to hunt.

These folks have not yet figured out that the toughest part of hunting mature modern-day mule deer bucks is simply finding where they live. To locate the areas with the best potential for a successful hunt, you need to become a researcher.

The consistently successful mule deer hunter in the 21st century will be the man or woman who knows that while the actual deer season may last for just a week or two, the "hunt" will take 52 weeks. It will begin in the dead of winter and encompass many bits and pieces of your time from then until you finally arrive on site and set up your tent, or meet your outfitter and prepare to head to his camp or ranch. The successful mule deer hunter will scout "around the clock," looking for the pot of gold at the end of the rainbow that can be traded for an isolated pocket of country in which bucks with eye-popping antlers live.

To find these pockets, you need information. There are lots of places to get it. In this chapter you'll learn ways to find a good place to hunt on your own, and recommendations on how to go about selecting an outfitter. Later in this book you'll find telephone and fax numbers and World Wide Web site addresses for government offices that can help you too, as well as places to find the maps you'll need.

Modern mule deer hunting is anything but a no-brainer. You need some luck, too. But you get lucky by planning and researching. Here's how to go about it …

RESEARCH: THE KEY TO SUCCESS

The key to any serious mule deer hunter's consistent, year-after-year success can be summarized in three short words—*planning* and *hard work*. Most of us get so fired up about the actual hunt itself that it's easy to forget that without proper planning and lots of research, the hunt is doomed from day one. Without pre-hunt research, once in the mountains any success is as much the result of blind luck as skill.

I'm not willing to leave my success to chance. That's why I'm a researcher.

All big game hunters tend to forget that before they can shoot an animal, they first have to find one. And finding a good muley or blacktail buck is by far the hardest part of the entire equation. Only very small pockets of habitat hold mulies at any given time, despite that the entire drainage might be good deer habitat. With limited hunting time, we all need to maximize the time we spend afield where the deer are, not where they might be. Research gets you there. Here's a step-by-step process.

STEP ONE: CREATE FILES

In my home office I have several files that help me plan my hunts. Into my "mule deer" file each year go all sorts of things—magazine articles, maps, harvest statistics, state game statistics, notes from books, etc. I also have separate files for each mule deer and blacktail state, into which go the coming year's hunting regulations and license and tag application procedures. These items help me decide on new areas I might want to hunt, based on information about what's hot, and what's not.

Keeping everything in a file folder it makes it easier for me to keep track of the several different hunting trips I'm planning for the coming year, and hunts I'm dreaming about for future years.

STEP TWO: CONTACT GAME DEPARTMENTS

Contact the game departments of the states you're considering and get the coming year's regulations. Deer seasons vary widely by state, as do application procedures, due dates and costs. And these days, it seems like states change the way they do things every year. The regulation booklets describe these changes.

Ask the department if it has harvest statistics and tag-drawing odds summaries available; many states do, for a slight fee. Spend the money and get one for each state. These numbers help paint a broad portrait of hunter success and distribution, harvest by area, tag-drawing odds and trophy quality.

STEP THREE: MAPS, MAPS, MAPS

Once you narrow your choice of a hunting area down to a general location, it's time for maps. The U.S. Forest Service and Bureau of Land Management each have public land maps within specific states that help you locate boundaries, roads, water sources, timbered ridges, trails and trail heads, campgrounds and more. I like general state maps too, which show major roads and towns. Together all these maps give me a good overview of the area I want to hunt.

Later in the process it will be time for U.S. Geological Survey (USGS) topographic maps. These maps show too small an area for initial planning, but are essential for the final planning and hunt execution phases of your trip, so hold off on buying them just yet. I use the larger maps to help me define the general area I want to hunt, then topo maps to show me exactly where the elk will be in the area, as well as how I will both access and attack the area.

I can't emphasize the importance of maps enough, both in planning and the actual hunt itself. Without them I feel as blind as the proverbial bat.

By using a topographic map of a potential hunting area when speaking with game department personnel, you're more apt to get concise, useful information than by just asking random, general questions.

STEP FOUR: PEOPLE WHO NEED PEOPLE

The final stage of the planning process is talking with people. Maps give you a general overview of the area, but people can fill in the blanks and give you an accurate, up-to-the-minute picture of what the area is really like.

"Up-to-date" is the key phrase here. While maps are invaluable, you rarely find one that's up-to-date. New roads, towns, subdivisions, trails, logging operations and fires, may not be shown on maps, but local people know about them and may help you fill in the blanks.

Talk with state game department biologists whenever possible. When I talk to these folks, I work my way down, not up, the departmental flow chart. I don't want the man in charge of half the state—I want the local biologist for a specific forest or drainage I'm considering hunting. The same holds true for game wardens, forest service personnel and so on. These people work right in the area, and can fill me in on current conditions and deer population numbers. They may be hard to locate, and it might take several phone calls to actually hook up with them once you've found out who they are, but it is time and money well spent. Also, these people might be aware of any local ranchers who may offer access to hunt their property for trespass fees. Always ask about this.

Whenever possible, I also talk with local hunters, taxidermists and any other meaningful contacts. I ask as many people as possible the same question, then "balance" their answers in my mind.

STEP FIVE: USGS TOPOGRAPHIC MAPS

About the time I call people, I buy topographic maps of the drainages I'm pretty sure I'm going to hunt. Topo maps help me pinpoint specific creeks, drainages and ridges where my research tells me the

Topo maps help you plan your hunt before you ever reach a new area. Use them both as a research tool and a navigation aid when the season finally opens.

Researching Potential Trophy Hot Spots

The three biological factors mentioned earlier in this book (see page 131) all come into play when researching areas to hunt trophy mule deer bucks. It's a two-step process. First, you find an area that holds the kind of deer you're hunting. Then, you hunt them in a way that maximizes your odds of seeing them during legal shooting hours.

Finding an area that holds trophy deer today—not yesterday—is the most difficult task faced by hunters. By systematically approaching the problem and breaking the search process down into pieces, it becomes easier to put the puzzle together. I call the process "shrinking your focus."

You shrink the area you'll be hunting down to a manageable, realistic piece of ground that you can hunt thoroughly. Step one is selecting a state to hunt. Then, by a process of elimination, choosing a single mountain range in that state. Next, select a small area of that often-vast mountain range, from which specific drainages are chosen. The final step is deciding at what elevation, and in what kind of cover, those drainages are hunted.

Trophy buck hunters don't approach this process willy-nilly. Most look for a new trophy deer hot spot 24 hours a day, 365 days a year. They discover that the key to finding such a spot is information.

To that end, I begin the area search process by reading. I read magazine articles and books, and I watch videos. I contact game departments and ask for data on deer—harvest data, buck/doe ratios, population data and so on. I also study both the Boone and Crockett and Pope and Young record books. These sources of information get me started by telling me historically where big bucks originate (meaning deer in these areas possess

The key to locating a trophy area is to "shrink your focus," reducing the area from a state to a mountain range, then down to a specific drainage in that mountain range, then deciding at what elevation and in what cover type you should begin hunting.

If so, has it affected the herd? What do deer eat in this area? What are their *preferred* food sources—those foods they will go out of their way to eat above all others? If I don't know what those plants look like, I go to the library and get a book that shows me, so I can identify them once I'm in the woods. Have there been any large fires? Timber cuttings? Large influx of cattle or sheep?

It's important to remember that, while an area that has produced record-class bucks in the past has the potential to do so at any given time, "hot" areas for big bucks can change seasonally. Several factors can influence this change. A subdivision set in the heart of winter range can crush a deer herd. Winter kill can pound almost any area of the Rockies. Fires that will produce tons of high-quality food in a year or two can destroy that same food while it burns. Increased predation—primarily by mountain lions, coyotes and bears—can decimate deer herds. And once the "word's out" on a given area, increased hunting pressure can dramatically cut into the area's number of large bucks.

That's why research and information are so important. Nothing is more frustrating than to head for a hunting area expecting the best, only to find that the hot spot you or someone you know hunted last year is now a golf course, ski resort or condo development. Because most of us do not live in trophy deer country, we have to do our research by telephone. We don't have the luxury of physically scouting all year, so we depend on our ability to gather information as our primary source of locating new areas to hunt. The more meticulous you are in your research, the better your chances of getting a look at the buck of your dreams.

the genetics to grow large antlers), as well as give me hard data on current herd status. Next I start talking to anybody and everybody that might give me a lead. Biologists, foresters, taxidermists, other hunters, ranchers, cowboys, sheep herders, backpackers, hunting guides and outfitters and others like them who are intimately familiar with a given area just might give me a lead. Naturally, I take everything with a grain of salt when talking with these people. Knowing that they might mislead me a bit, once I come across a promising tidbit of information, I try to confirm it by asking others their opinion about what I've heard. Only after I confirm it do I begin to get excited.

I always ask about food and water, as well as local range conditions. Has there been a drought?

deer should be when I arrive. Topo maps also allow me to ask the people I'm calling very specific questions about the area. I coat my topos with a clear waterproof sealer that I can write on, and I write notes on them during my research, detailing information I learn talking with people. Topo maps help me narrow things down from general information on the elk herd to specific terrain features, areas that may receive lots of pressure from other hunters, the best ways to access the hunting grounds and so on. When I'm done with my research, my topo maps closely resemble those used in military operations.

Research. I know it's more like school than hunting, and it sure isn't as much fun as spotting a wide, heavy-antlered buck on a frosty fall morning. But it's all part of the chess game, a way to tip the odds for success in your favor, and a way to keep the fire burning during the off-season. You get to talk hunting with other folks, probably even make some new friends.

No, it's not foolproof. That's why they call this sport we love "hunting." But it sure beats stumbling around the mountains like some clueless city boy waiting for the Prize Patrol to arrive with the envelope.

Scouting Around the Clock

If you live in or near mule deer or blacktail country, then you're a candidate to do what some of my serious buck hunting buddies do. That's "scout around the clock."

These folks look for new honey holes to hunt big bucks 365 days a year. They live and breathe it. And they're a little bit crazy too. For example, I have friends who live in southern California and hunt Arizona, Utah and Nevada when they can draw a tag. They think nothing of leaving after work Friday night, driving hundreds of miles, scouting all day Saturday and Sunday morning, driving hundreds of miles home, and going back to work on Monday morning. Closer to home, they talk their wives or girlfriends into going "hiking" with them for the weekend. Of course they like to hike into potential new honey holes for big bucks. In spring you find them on the winter range, shed hunting.

When they're not on the ground scouting, they're talking deer hunting to anyone and everyone who will talk back to them. They develop a knack for gleaning information from people without giving away their own secrets. It's an art.

Some folks call these people nuts. Kooks. Insane. I call them dedicated buck hunters. More often than not, scouting around the clock pays big dividends for them. It can do the same for you too.

"Scouting around the clock" includes shed hunting, as well as gathering information all year long that pertains to a potential new mule deer honey hole.

HOW TO BOOK A GUIDED HUNT

I've been on more than my share of guided hunts of all types since my first—an elk hunt in the early 1980s. Most have been excellent. Unfortunately, some have not. The question is, how can you assure that a mule deer hunt you booked will be a everything you expected, and not a tangled, unpleasant mess?

ONE WORD: RESEARCH

Every year I meet excited hunters who book with the first outfitter they meet, believing the hype and hoopla, and plunking their money down without doing any comparison shopping. Sometimes these

trips turn out great. Often they are less than ideal. Quite honestly, a number of outfitters out there are slicker than a snake oil salesman, fudging the facts so they can get into your wallet. These guys show you lots of pictures of big bucks, giving you the impression that such success is routine. They forget to tell you the last time they killed one like that Nixon was president, bell bottoms were hip, and gas cost 30 cents a gallon.

First, you must have realistic expectations about a guided hunting trip. Remember that booking a guided trip does not guarantee you'll harvest an animal, let alone a record-class buck. What it should guarantee is that you'll be provided with solid food, a comfortable camp, a guide who knows his stuff and is willing to work hard, and the opportunity to hunt an area where you have a reasonably good chance of finding the animal you desire. Before contacting prospective outfitters, there are some questions you need to answer honestly about why you want to go on a guided hunt. These questions apply to all guided hunting, not just trips for mule deer.

• *What animal do you* really *want to hunt?* Sounds basic, but many people do not target a single species as their priority. If hunting big mulies is your goal, with an elk secondary, but nice if one happens along, you want to choose an outfitter in an area with lots of deer, not one in an area with lots of elk but just a few mule deer.

• *Is taking an animal more important than the quality of the experience?* If so, you're setting yourself up for disappointment. Even the best guides and outfitters have weeks where the animals and/or weather don't

cooperate. If an outfitter historically has gotten 75 percent of his clients an animal, you just might be in the 25 percent that year who return empty-handed. There are no guarantees for success in fair-chase hunting. The best you can do is play the odds—and there are places where the chances for success are better than others.

• *Are you willing to do what it takes to prepare for the hunt?* You can't expect to take a good buck on a tough backpack hunt if you are not in good physical condition to make it up and down the mountain. Will you take time before the hunt to practice with your weapon, so that when your one good opportunity during a week's hunt presents itself you are able to take advantage of it? The inability to walk rough terrain and shoot with proficiency are the two most common complaints outfitters have about clients.

• *What type of camp and hunting style will make you happy?* Is camping in a small backpack tent okay with

Finding the right guide and outfitter—one that can help you make your mule deer hunting dreams come true—takes time and research, and requires you to be honest with yourself about your hunting goals.

Mule Deer—Western Challenge

Magazines (like North American Hunter), *and the* NAHC Resource Directory, *are great places to start your search for an outfitter. Continue your homework after initial calls are made.*

you, or do you prefer the comfort of a lodge with a soft bed? Would you prefer to hunt while floating a river, or hiking among the peaks? Do you mind riding horses? Does treestand hunting bore you, or is this what you prefer? Be honest with yourself, or you'll end up being miserable.

Only after being honest with yourself is it time to seek out individual outfitters. There are several ways to do this. I've met lots of top outfitters at some of the major hunting and fishing shows held around the country. Sport shows are a great place to interact personally with outfitters and have many of your questions answered on the spot. Advertisements in the back of magazines like *North American Hunter* are another source. Using a booking agent who represents several different outfitters is one way to help short-cut the research process. Word of mouth from friends who have hunted with a particular outfit is perhaps your best source of information.

Finally, give yourself enough time to plan your trip, locate a suitable outfitter and set aside vacation time.

Most top outfitters book the majority of their hunts a year or more in advance. Rushing the process is a good way to make a mistake that could turn your dream into endless grief.

10 QUESTIONS YOU MUST ASK

Before any money changes hands, ask prospective outfitters the following 10 questions:

1 What animals do you hunt? What are the species with top trophy potential in your area? If you want a muley buck, with an average elk as your secondary goal, but the area has only mediocre bucks and lots of elk, you're probably hunting in the wrong place.

2 How many actual hunting days will I have? On a 10-day hunt, you might have one day travel time each way, in and out of the hunting area, cutting the actual hunt time to eight days. If you're stranded in base camp for extra days because the outfitter has

Hunting Homework: The Outfitter-Client Relationship

Jim Van Norman and successful hunter Tom Nelson.

A guided hunt can be a satisfying experience for both the hunter and the outfitter/guide. In fact, the relationship that grows from the business deal may turn into a lifetime friendship. Here are a few tips on how to get ready for such a hunt—some things to expect from an outfitter and some things that might be expected of you.

First—always book a hunt that has been recommended by someone you know, a person who has been to the camp. Calling cold turkey and booking a hunt with just any outfitter is risky business! There are a lot of good outfitters out there; unfortunately, there are also some who are just plain bad at it, and some who are downright dishonest. References are a *must*. Make the phone calls and ask some detailed questions about the outfitter, his camp and the guides. It's cheap insurance when you are spending a good chunk of money for a hunt.

A GOOD OUTFITTER ON A FULL-SERVICE HUNT SHOULD PROVIDE, AS THE BASICS, THE FOLLOWING:

—Accommodations for comfortable sleeping. This doesn't necessarily mean that the outfitter provides the bedding. There's a good chance you may be asked to bring your own sleeping bag. But the sleeping quarters should keep the weather out and have the facilities, including adequate supplies, to keep the place warm and reasonably comfortable.

—Three meals a day. This generally consists of *at least* a continental breakfast, a good-sized lunch (usually in the field), snacks and a big evening meal.

—A knowledgeable guide. Two hunters per guide is normal on a mule deer hunt, but you may be better served to go one-on-one (usually for an extra fee).

—Meat and trophy care. These should be provided prior to transport to the processor. The processing costs, once the meat is in town, and the taxidermy fees, are the responsibility of the hunter (unless otherwise arranged).

Most reputable outfitters ask for a 50 percent deposit on the hunt at booking and for the balance to be paid either 7 to 14 days prior to the hunt or upon arrival.

Prices on mule deer hunts vary throughout the industry based on the quality of the outfitter and the quality of the camp, as well as the quality and availability of trophies.

HERE ARE A FEW THINGS THE OUTFITTER MAY EXPECT FROM YOU:

—That you are in reasonably good physical condition. Your fitness level needs to be in proportion to the type of hunt you're going on—a pack-in trip to timberline is a lot more rigorous than a ranch hunt. But in either situation, taking someone hunting who may be jeopardizing his own life is not enjoyable for an outfitter/guide, and usually is an unwelcome hardship on both the hunter and the outfitter's crew. I know this from first-hand experience. Plus, quartering and packing out a huge dead person is a tough job! All jokes aside—get in good shape before your hunt; you'll enjoy the overall experience far more, and you'll get a better buck to boot.

—That you are proficient with your weapon. Take the time to become a good shot regardless of the nature of your projectile—centerfire bullet, broadhead-tipped arrow or muzzleloader ball. The whole hunt may come down to a one-shot opportunity, so you need to be ready. Also, take time to fix and maintain your equipment. Nothing is more frustrating, for both outfitter and hunter, than to have an equipment malfunction back in the boondocks—with no one having the foggiest idea of how to repair it.

—That you are prepared for all kinds of weather. Through proper communication, whether it be by letter or telephone, your outfitter should instruct you on what clothes and other gear to bring, including footgear. Autumn weather in the Great American West is unpredictable at best. Weather conditions vary widely and can change instantly for the worse (or, yes, the better).

Hunter and guide, dragging out a good buck.

—That you pay promptly, as discussed or contracted between outfitter and client during booking. This is just good business and simply shows good faith. Remember, your outfitter will be your friend and wants to have fun too, but this is how the outfitter and his or her employees make a living.

—That you are willing to listen and take heed of suggestions. Hunters these days are well-traveled, but when you hire someone to take you hunting—that person is the expert. Since the outfitter or guide spends a considerable amount of time in the hunting area, there's more than a good chance that he or she knows more than you do about the land and the mulies that live there—regardless of your overall experience. A good outfitter/guide recognizes your abilities and knowledge in time and generally asks your opinion often. In other words, respect his or her knowledge. They wouldn't be highly recommended if they didn't know their stuff.

At my outfit, if we encounter a "know it all," who is also hard to get along with (as is usual in this case), we spend the first two hunt days on some sort of a "death march" or our friend is promptly put into the "penalty stand" where no buck has been seen since the last wagon train went through. These practices are more commonly referred to as "piss and vinegar cleansing treks" or "attitude adjustment stints." Hunters who listen, get pumped, hunt hard—they go immediately to the big buck pastures. Do other outfitters do this? It's your call.

FINAL WORD: HOMEWORK

There's not room to cover everything here, but these ideas give you the basics and take some of the mystery out of booking a hunt. When a few people get together (outfitter, guide, hunter) and spend a considerable amount of time together as a team—hunting, stalking, laughing and sharing the outdoors—a bond is always formed. It will happen every time—as long as everyone does his homework!

—Jim Van Norman

problems, will he allow you to extend your hunt to compensate for missed days afield that were not your fault? The outfitter can't control the weather, but he should be in control of his equipment, staff and scheduling.

3 *How many hunters and support people will there be in camp?* To avoid overcrowding, you want to know how many other hunters will be in hunting camp. Also ask if your guide doubles as the cook, horse wrangler and wood cutter. Generally, but not always, it's better if the guide does nothing except take you hunting.

4 *How many hunters per guide?* Do you have your guide all to yourself, or will you be sharing him with another client? Though it costs more, it's almost always more productive to hunt one-on-one. If you get to camp and your one-on-one hunt is suddenly a two-on-one affair, immediately solve the problem with the outfitter.

5 *How long have you been hunting in your area?* I prefer to hunt with people who have been outfitting an area for at least three seasons, and therefore, know the area and area game movements well.

6 *How long have your guides worked for you?* The outfitter rarely will take you hunting himself. You want a guide with experience hunting both the area and species you're targeting. Don't settle for a first-year guide as your primary guide.

7 *For you bowhunters: Are your guides experienced bowhunters themselves?* Have they successfully guided bowhunters before? Very important for bowhunters is a guide who understands the unique requirements of hunting with archery tackle. There are few non-bowhunters who make good bowhunting guides.

8 *What percentage of your clients are repeat customers?* If the outfitter was lousy and there was no game in the area, he probably wouldn't have many repeat clients. Repeat business is a good indicator of a reputable outfit.

9 *What does the hunt package cost?* You'll be quoted a hunt cost of, say, $4,000 for a guided mule deer hunt. Now ask about any "hidden" costs like licenses and tags (rarely included in the hunt price), trophy and meat care, tips and gratuities, additional charges if you take another animal and so on. Is there a "trophy fee" for harvesting an animal, or for taking an animal that scores exceptionally well by record-book standards? These "extras" can add hundreds of dollars to a hunt's base price. No one likes to be surprised.

10 *Do you have references I can contact?* Ask not only for a list of successful clients, but also clients who did not get game on their hunt. Ask for references within the last three years. Spend a few bucks and call them all, and ask lots of questions regarding all aspects of the hunt. If an outfitter won't provide references, avoid him like the plague.

Big Bucks for Big Bucks

Private-land ranch hunts may be your best bet for a truly big mule deer these days.

"The most expensive hunts we've booked in several years, regardless of species, are mule deer hunts," says Garth Carter of Garth Carter's Hunter Services (435)386-1020 (or on the Web at www.huntinfool.com). Carter runs a booking agency and information service that helps hunters learn where the best opportunities are for top-quality western big game hunting. "The demand for trophy-class mule deer today is huge, simply because they are so hard to come by. On one private land hunt, we sold mule deer hunts for $20,000 each, and everyone expected a chance at a buck scoring at least 190 Boone and Crockett points."

"Ranchers that are managing for trophy mulies—I'm talking about true trophy hunts, where you can have a good chance at shooting either a buck scoring 185 B&C or better, or a buck with a 30-inch spread—run somewhere between $5,000 and $10,000," Carter says. "Outfitters who hunt private land and have a track record of producing these kind of bucks have a waiting list for these hunts at these prices."

"While I still believe you can kill the best buck in the world with the right special-draw tag on public land, you can up your odds by booking a private ranch hunt," Carter said. In most cases, Carter recommends looking for ranches with hunts that begin on or after November 1, when the rut is starting and the deer are beginning to move out of the thick cover and onto more open lower-elevation country, where they are more easily spotted.

BASIC FIELD CARE

As we've seen, mule deer hunting is hard work. Heck, just finding a good buck is a chore. So when it all comes together and you're walking up to your buck and your heart is soaring like a hawk, the last thing on your mind is what to do next.

But your hunt is anything but over. Now comes the dirty work. It's time to care for this hard-earned meat, a most welcome addition to my freezer each fall. If you are really lucky, perhaps this is a buck that will grace a wall in your home or office. To make sure that both the meat and the cape and antlers make it back to civilization in excellent shape, you have to know how to care for them properly.

That all starts with a basic knowledge of field dressing your deer, then cooling the meat to prevent a tainted, "gamey" taste or even spoilage, regardless of whether the temperature is 100°F or below freezing. It's a simple chore, really, but one that requires the right tools and an understanding of the proven, step-by-step procedures that work for thousands of buck hunters every fall.

And while caping a deer head might seem like brain surgery to someone who hasn't done it before, it really isn't all that tough. Once you understand what has to be done and remember that you're not racing anyone to the finish, but instead can take all the time you want to make sure you're doing it right, it is relatively easy.

Last fall I was fortunate enough to shoot a pretty nice buck. As I walked up to him, the feeling of accomplishment and satisfaction was great. I sat next to him for a moment and watched the world go by, thinking that I was one of the luckiest men alive to be in that spectacular place on such a beautiful day. As I held his dark, polished antlers in my hands I gave thanks for this magnificent deer. Those feelings were enhanced when I reached for my knife and began field dressing him. The weight of his meat, cape and antlers on my back as I hiked to my camp, though heavy, felt good.

Caring for game is a privilege—something I both enjoy and take seriously. If you do the deed, you owe it to the animal to make sure that it is taken care of properly. Here's how to do the job ...

FIELD DRESSING & MEAT CARE

*I*f you hunt deer long enough, sooner or later you'll be fortunate enough to take care of one in the field. Many sportsmen and women don't like to clean their deer and care for the meat. I love doing it. To me, it is the culmination of a lot of planning and hard work, a privilege that I savor. Some of my friends get it over with as quickly as possible. On the other hand, unless poor conditions—rain, snow, coming darkness, a long, tough pack through bad country—dictate that I have to hurry, I like to take my time. I perform my own autopsy, seeing what damage my bullet or broadhead did, learning as much as I can that will help me place my shot better the next time.

There is no single right and wrong way to field dress a deer. Anyone who has done more than one develops their own method. It really isn't very difficult.

THE RIGHT TOOLS

Meat care begins with the right tools. For mule hunting, you will need razor-sharp hunting knife with a strong blade. You don't need a Bowie knife to dress a deer. I've done it with a small pocket knife or the knife blade from a multi-tool. Better still is a hunting knife with a clip-point blade between 4 and 6 inches long, with a handle made of either bone or a no-slip material like Zytel. You'll need a sharpening stone or steel. A lightweight saw or hatchet for splitting the brisket and cutting off the antlers comes in handy, although you can split a deer's brisket easily with the serrated blade featured on many multi-blade folding hunting knives. About 50 feet of nylon parachute cord comes in handy, as do a pair of large, heavy-duty, washable cotton meat sacks. Don't get the *el cheapo* cheesecloth meat sacks, but buy the ones that are heavy enough to be washed and reused. The best I've ever used are from The Alaska Game Bag (907/376-8476, e-mail: akna@ alaska.net) and cost less than a 10-spot for a four-pack. Be sure to have at least one roll of fluorescent flagging and/or your GPS unit, so you can mark the kill site in case you have to come back for subsequent trips. A head lamp is cheap at twice the price when you have to butcher a deer after dark.

Your goal is to prevent meat spoilage. You do that by cooling the meat, remembering that meat spoils both from the inside and outside. You also must keep the meat as clean as possible, free from dirt and its inherent bacteria.

SECURE THE DEER

Before any cutting begins, you have to secure the deer, which often has expired on a steep side hill. That's where the parachute cord comes in. I use it to tie antlers or legs to a tree or bush to hold the animal in place as I work. Whenever possible, though, I lay the deer almost level. Point the butt downhill a bit if possible. Butchering a deer is much easier with two people, so if you can get some help, do it.

FIELD DRESSING BASICS

There are two ways to clean any big game animal, including deer. You can do the basic field-dressing routine, which means first gutting the animal. Or you can take the quarters, backstrap and neck off without gutting. I do either, depending on circumstances.

The basic field-dressing procedure is the same with mule deer as it is with other big game. I first remove the lower legs just below the knees, taking care to not cut through the hamstring. Find the correct joint, and the legs come off as slick as you please. Next I remove the innards, including the anus, taking care not to puncture the bladder or stomach and spilling their contents onto the meat; suffice it to say this is not a good idea. I work from the rear of the deer, first pinching a little skin just in front of the penis, then carefully slicing through it, with the sharp edge of the knife pointing up. I extend this slit up to the sternum, then return and continue it from the penis sheath to the anus. I try not to puncture the mesenteric tissue on this pass with the knife, using the first cut as more of a guide for the upcoming serious stuff.

When cutting through the mesenteric tissue, keep the knife blade up, using the index and middle fingers of your non-cutting hand to shield the bulging organs from the blade point as you slice forward to the sternum. Because the juices of the paunch will almost always taint the meat, if I happen to accidentally slice the innards, or if the bullet or broadhead has cut them open and they are leaking, I work quickly to try and

A sharp hunting knife, and a lightweight saw for removing antlers and splitting the brisket, are the basic tools of field care. A small hatchet can also come in handy.

minimize the amount of juices that flow onto the meat.

Before removing the innards, I core the anus, working from the rear of the deer and cutting around it in a circular fashion. Usually you have to finish the job from the inside of the deer, so I push the paunch forward and finish the job from inside the cavity, again taking care not to slit the paunch. I cut the penis off close to the anus, slicing both it and the testicles free and discarding them. Pull the anus into the body cavity; now all the innards will come easily out of the body cavity. I keep the deer on its back and roll them out, which helps keep dirt, sticks and other debris off the meat. Pull the anus through from the inside, if it doesn't come out with everything else. I then remove the liver, carefully cutting it free and placing it in a half-gallon heavy-duty zip-top bag I carry in my hunting pack for this purpose.

Next it's time to remove the heart, lungs and esophagus. You first cut around the diaphragm. This is usually bloody work, because proper bullet or broadhead placement destroys the lungs. If the deer is on its back and positioned slightly downhill, much of it runs out through the anus. At this point I find it helpful to cut directly through the sternum, using either my pack saw or the serrated blade from my multi-blade hunting knife. (NOTE: Don't do this if you're going to cape the deer for a mount!) This

Prompt and proper field dressing is the first step to good venison.

makes removing the lungs and heart much easier. I cut them off as close to the throat as possible. I may or may not save the heart; if I do, it goes into the same zip-top bag as the liver.

To drain the blood from the chest cavity, simply lift the deer up by the front half and let it drain out the anus. If there's snow on the ground, you can use some of it to wipe the cavity down.

QUARTER OR BONE IT OUT?

I field dress a buck when I can't finish the job right away, when I might have to leave the carcass to cool overnight or for several hours before packing it out. When I do this I lay the animal on its back, then cut the front shoulders so they lay away from the carcass, and cut the hams to the ball joint, so they too, are opened up enough to cool down. I reach up into the throat and cut out the esophagus. I often use a stick to prop open the chest cavity so air circulates freely.

However, because I usually hunt rough country and rarely am able to get the carcass out whole, these days I prefer to quarter the animal without exposing his guts. It's less messy and smelly, and I don't lose any

meat. I can then either pack the quarters, or bone the meat off them, before loading my packframe up and heading down off the mountain.

To do that, first roll the deer on one side and use your knife to remove the hind quarter through the ball joint, then the front shoulder by cutting behind the scapula. Next remove the backstrap, half the neck meat and the meat off the outside of the rib cage, or, if you like, use your saw to cut the ribs completely off. (I rarely do this.) You then roll the buck over and repeat. To get the tenderloins out—they're located inside the carcass on each side of the backbone—use your serrated knife blade or your lightweight saw to cut through the tops of the rib cage and remove them this way. When ready for bagging, skin the quarters out. *Voila!* One butchered buck, without the big mess of field dressing it first.

I virtually always bone my deer meat out, for two reasons. One, it gets rid of excess weight that I don't have to pack down the mountain. And two, removing the bone opens the meat up and facilitates cooling. Thick chunks of meat, like those found on the hams and neck, spoil quickly near the bone unless they are properly cooled. Boning helps this process. Hunters

Mule Deer—Western Challenge

with the luxury of pack horses often like to keep the bone in, because it makes loading quarters into pack boxes easier.

SHOULD YOU WASH THE MEAT?

Some hunters still believe that getting their deer meat wet ruins it. On the contrary, washing the meat thoroughly with cold water is one of the best things you can do to ensure tender, flavorful table fare.

When I get back to civilization, if my deer is quartered—or by some miracle, still a whole carcass—I hang it up and wash it using a garden hose. I wash and wash until all traces of blood, bone chips, dirt and grime are gone. I also trim it up at this time, cutting away any bloodshot meat. If I can't hang the meat or if no hose is available, I'll use creek water. I've been known to wash my meat in a motel room bathroom from time to time.

After washing, let the meat drip dry. If you have some clean old towels or rags and can pat it dry, so much the better. Hang it in muslin bags to keep the bugs off as it dries. When it does, you're ready to cut and wrap it for the freezer.

That's all there is to it. Field dressing a buck is not rocket science. But it does take the proper tools and some careful cutting to do the job right. And somehow, dressing a deer you've taken yourself just makes the meat taste all the sweeter come suppertime.

Why You Should Wear Gloves

One year in Alaska, I shot a huge brown bear. During the skinning process I got careless, deeply cutting the index finger of my left hand. A few days later I was on Kodiak Island, where the Sitka blacktail hunting is superb. I butchered several deer the first couple of days before the infection set in. The area where I had cut my finger became red and swollen. Soon it was so painful I hardly could stand it.

We weren't picked up by the air taxi service for four more days. When we got back to the town of Kodiak, I went straight to the hospital. The antibiotics they gave me didn't work, and the swelling kept getting bigger and more painful. Back home I was lucky enough to have as my neighbor an old-timer who had been a doctor in Alaska for decades. Right away he recognized the problem, and gave me the strongest antibiotics he could prescribe. I'll never forget his words when I asked him what the prognosis was. "Well, son," he said, "this will either cure it or we'll be taking that finger right off."

Fortunately, the drugs worked. But my finger is trashed. It gets so white and cold now in moderate temperatures it has me wondering just how bad it will be in 20 more years. All because I was careless skinning and butchering game.

For that reason, I never field dress deer anymore without wearing a pair of rubber gloves to protect my hands from possible infection. I don't wear those thin little throwaway surgical gloves most people use—if they use any at all. Instead, I wear either heavy-duty rubber fisherman's gloves or super heavy-duty kitchen gloves. I take care to not nick them with my knife while I'm working. Once I'm done with the meat-care chores, I vigorously wash my hands with soap and clean water.

You have a choice. You can either wear gloves when field dressing game, or roll the dice and risk infection. It's your fingers. Me? Let's just say that I don't want anyone ever calling me "Stumpy."

HOT WEATHER MEAT CARE

*I*n some parts of the West, mule deer seasons open early. Very early. So early that daytime temperatures can soar into the stratosphere. For example, rifle hunting along the central California coast opens in early August (bow season opens in July), when temperatures routinely top 100°F. Many other early bow seasons throughout the West are conducted during hot weather too.

Improper meat care in hot weather can lead to tainted meat or, even worse, spoilage. Unless you take care of your deer properly, the fruits of your success can wind up at the local dump.

"In order to make the best products from your wild game, we need to start with game that was well taken care of in the field," said Doug Drum, proprietor of Indian Valley Meats in Indian, Alaska. Drum, who grew up around a slaughterhouse in Michigan, has a business that processes between 275,000 and 300,000 pounds of meat each year.

"There are many theories as to how to take care of meat in the field," Drum said. "I use a proven method that is based on the principles used in the meat processing industry. The aim of this method is to make life harder for bacteria and flies by creating a cool, high-acid environment to slow their growth, limiting their food sources by bleaching out blood, making a protective glaze coating and controlling flies."

Use the Right Game Bag

Drum advises hunters never to use game bags made from either plastic or woven plastic, because they tend to hold in heat and don't permit proper air circulation. He recommends using cheesecloth-type game bags, or those made from a cheesecloth-type material. These are strong enough to carry the meat, yet allow for maximum air circulation. They are also tight enough to keep the flies out.

Drum also advises sportsmen and women to treat their game bags with a citric acid blend. "While the flies may light on a bag treated with a citric acid solution, the citric acid burns them, and they won't hang around long," Drum said. "The citric acid also helps inhibit bacteria growth.

"To understand how this works, you must first understand that bacteria grows rapidly at a pH level of 7.0," Drum said. "The pH contained in lemons or limes is about 2.35. By using a citric-acid solution on the bag, the pH level drops dramatically, helping kill bacteria." You can make your own citric acid solution by combining the juice of three lemons, one large bottle of lemon juice concentrate and one small bottle of Tabasco sauce. Soak the game bag in this solution for 20 minutes to one hour, then let them air dry completely (not in your dryer!) Then store them in zip-top bags.

Cooling the Meat

The sooner your meat is cooled down, the better it will be. It is important to quickly bleed, gut and skin the animal as soon as possible. Next you should reduce the carcass temperature.

If you're near a stream or lake, you can safely dunk the meat in the cool water to bring the temperature down. However, Drum cautioned not to cool the meat completely in the water, but instead allow the meat to retain just enough heat so that it will dry itself once it comes out of the water.

Air Drying/Storing Meat in the Field

After the meat temperature is lowered, it's important to air dry the meat, Drum said. "The key is to hang the meat out of direct sunlight in the shade, where any breeze will gently blow across the carcass," he said. "Excess moisture can be squeegeed off the

Use game bags made of cheesecloth-type material to keep flies and dirt off your carcass or meat, yet allow air circulation and cooling.

meat with your hands, or wiped away with clean paper or cloth towels.

"Once the excess moisture is removed, apply the same lemon juice mixture mentioned earlier in a light coat over the entire carcass," Drum said. "This creates a high-acid protective glaze over the meat while it is drying." Once the meat is dry, it can be placed in game bags and rehung.

The Fly Trap

In many areas, flies are a problem with game carcasses. The solution is to build a small fly trap near the place where you've hung the carcass to glaze over and cool.

"All it takes to build a fly trap is a can of Golden Malprin—available at many feed and mill stores—and a black garbage bag," Drum said. "Eight to 10 feet away from the meat, lay a couple of branches on the ground. Pile meat scraps on and around the branches. Pour the Golden Malprin on and around the scraps of meat. Cut a slit in the center of the garbage bag, then place it loosely over the pile."

"The sun will heat up the plastic, which in turn heats the meat," Drum said. "The flies are attracted to the whole mess, and crawl in through the slit in the plastic. The Golden Malprin kills the flies. When you're ready to leave the area, put the whole trap into a zip-top bag, carry it from the field, and properly dispose of it."

TROPHY CARE

If you plan on having a head-and-shoulder mount of your buck created, you need to cape the head rather than randomly skin the animal. Some hunters like to save capes anyway, selling them to their taxidermist. Regardless, a knowledge of the basic fundamentals of caping is useful.

CAPING CONSIDERATIONS

Because deer heads are relatively small, you can cape the animal one of two basic ways. The first is where it lays after you've shot it in the field. On back-pack hunts and other times when you can't get some

sort of transportation to the animal—horses, ATV or truck—this sometimes makes sense. Packing a boned-out deer is tough enough over broken, steep ground. Eliminating the weight and bulk of the skull and excess meat helps make that job easier.

Generally speaking, however, you'll probably want to remove the head with the cape and antlers intact and transport it to a more controlled location, where you can take your time to finish the job. Another good option is to remove the head and cape as described, but take them to your taxidermist, who will professionally cape it out for a small fee.

I've found it much easier and neater to partially cape a deer and remove his head before I do the much messier meat care chores. This helps keep blood and gunk off both my hands and the cape. However, if the weather is hot, I partially field dress the deer before caping. To do this, I make a small incision from the penis sheath to a few inches shy of the breast bone, then core the anus. My purpose it to create a hole in the belly just large enough for me to reach in and remove the digestive system, then drain the blood through the anus, away from the cape. I then skin the carcass up to the head, remove the head and cape at the atlas joint, and set it aside to work on after I finish caring for the meat.

REMOVING HEAD & CAPE

Beginning with the head, make a 45-degree diagonal cut from the base of the back side of each antler to the centerline of the neck, which results in a Y-shaped cut in the back of the head. I then make an incision down the middle of the neck and along the center of the backline, using the backbone as a guide.

Remember that you need to leave lots of hide for the taxidermist to work with. I run the cut down the backbone approximately 18 to 24 inches behind the front shoulder. I then cut on a line parallel with the front leg, stopping at the belly line (or the slit I made in the belly to remove the innards.) This may seem like a lot of extra hide, but I've never met a taxidermist yet who scolded a client for bringing in too much cape. But cut the cape too short, and he'll ream you. Guaranteed.

Next, skin out the front legs. Cut around each front leg just above the knee, then slit up to the torso along the back of the leg until it meets the chest cavity. Now carefully skin the deer forward, including the neck to

the base of the skull, taking care not to puncture the hide, but trying to remove all meat and fat. When finished, remove the head by using your knife to cut through the atlas joint, which is where the head swivels on the top of the neck. You don't need a saw or hatchet for this; your knife is enough.

CAPING DEER HEADS

Once the deer is skinned to the base of the skull, the easy part is over. Now you can lug it all out to the taxidermist to finish the job. But time or weather factors may dictate that you finish the job yourself. If so, here's how to cape the face and around the antlers.

Caping a deer head is not all that difficult. In the back-country, you may need to cape the head out yourself, a task that requires patience and a sharp, thin-bladed knife. Take your time around the eyes, ears, lips and nose, areas where it is easy to cut through the thin hide.

Caping–The Major Cuts

Here are the cuts to make to get the skin off your buck for a shoulder mount. In this scenario, you whack off the head and take the entire package to the taxidermist for the detail work of getting the skin off the buck's face. If you're patient and/or won't be able to get to a taxidermist in one day, or can't freeze the package, you'll have to do the detail work yourself, as described on page 173.

1 Cut through the hide around the deer's midsection, 4-6 inches behind the front legs. Extend the cut up the middle of the back to the deer's head. Divide the cut there, to the base of each antler.

2 Here are the cuts to make underneath. You can see the midsection cut. Cut the hide around each front leg, just above the knee, then cut

along the back of the legs to meet the cut around the midsection, as shown.

3 Skin the leg and body, working toward the head. Saw the head off or, if you don't have a saw, the atlas joint (marked with an X here) can be pried apart with your knife. Then roll the tube of skin up, tie it with a string under the deer's chin, and you're ready to hike out.

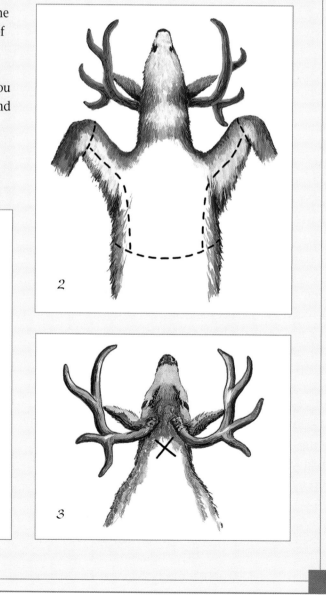

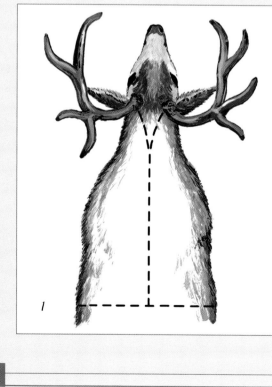

The first "problem" area comes when you reach the ears, which is also the time to remove the cape from around the base of each antler. It's tight here, and while you can do it with your knife if you're careful, a blunt object like a screwdriver (which acts as a small pry bar) makes it easy to pry the hide off cleanly around the burr. Now cut off the ears at their bases, taking care in keeping the knife blade as close as possible to the skull. This area is all cartilage, and the line to cut is easy to see and follow.

Continue skinning the head forward until you reach the eyes. This is the toughest part of any caping job. Keep the knife blade as close to the bone as possible, pull the eyelids gently upward from the outside, then carefully cut through the attaching membrane. Take care not to cut the eyelids. I like to slide a finger into the eye socket and lift the lid out, which helps avoid this. At the front of the eye you run into deep tear ducts. These must be carefully skinned deep inside the duct. A narrow-bladed pocket knife works well for this delicate chore.

Once through the eyes, continue working down the face, leaving a thick piece of cartilage on the skin at the nose. Make sure to cut the lips off well back inside the mouth. At this point the cape will come right off. If you will be in camp any length of time, especially in hot weather, you need to turn the ears inside out and split the lips. Ears are done by carefully skinning down into the ear itself, pushing from the underside with a blunt stick. Once you get them started you can sometimes use your finger or a blunt flat stick to work down into the ear and separate the cartilage from the skin. Once the ears are done you can turn them completely inside out. Splitting lips involves painstakingly slicing them open on the inside to promote cooling and permit all flesh removal. One word of caution, though: The skin inside the ears and around the lips is thin and easy to cut through. Take your time and work carefully in these areas.

During the caping process, remember to take your time and work only in short, flat strokes with the knife. If you slip and cut through the skin—don't panic, but don't make a habit of it. A good taxidermist can sew most small cuts up in such a way that you'll never know they were there.

Once the cape is removed, you can saw the antlers off the skull. All you do is cut the top of the skull off using your saw or hatchet. Sawing is easier if you first remove excess meat with your knife. To know where to cut, draw an imaginary line through the bottom third of the eye sockets parallel to the base of the antlers, and start sawing. Once this has been cut off, take a little time to remove any brain and eye matter, and cut away the biggest chunks of meat.

CARING FOR THE CAPE

Once the cape is off you have to keep it from spoiling, which would cause the hair to slip and fall out during the tanning process. There are two ways to do this: freezing and salting.

Most taxidermists I know like to receive frozen capes. When I know I can reach a freezer in short order—the exact time depends on the weather—I simply roll up my cape, place it in a heavy-duty plastic garbage bag (trash compactor bags are great for this), and put it in the freezer.

Salting is pretty simple too. It takes about four to five pounds of non-iodized salt to salt a mature mule deer cape adequately. Simply lay the cape on a flat surface, hair side down, and pour some salt onto the exposed skin. Diligently work the salt into every nook and cranny of the cape with your fingers, taking pains to get enough in the ear, eye, nose and lip areas. Using a pair of rubber gloves helps prevent salt from getting into all those little nicks and cuts you've gotten on your fingers and hands during the week. Once the hide is salted, roll it up and store it out of the sun.

The salt draws all the moisture out of the hide, causing the cape to produce a putrid liquid brine. After a salted cape has sat out overnight, it needs to be drained. I take my capes and lay them across a fence post, sagebrush bush or other similar object, hair side up, and allow it to drain for a bit. I then salt it again, remembering that salt is cheap and a ruined cape can't be replaced. Once salted, the cape is then rolled up, placed in a muslin game bag and stored in a cool, dry area.

Chapter 9

THE MULE DEER'S FUTURE

When I was a young boy, I read the work of Jack O'Connor in the pages of the dog-eared copies of *Outdoor Life* lying around the county fire station, where my dad worked. O'Connor captivated me with his tales of sheep hunting and marksmanship, of traveling to far-off places and having adventures that seemed, to me anyway, that he was almost on the moon.

It was his tales of hunting the deer of the West, though, that deeply hooked me. Pictures of Jack and his wife, Eleanor, posing with large-racked muley bucks taken with his old .270—the same kind of rifle my dad had, the rifle with which I took my first deer—grabbed me like a giant's hands. At the age of eight, I knew that I was going to be a buck hunter, just like my dad and O'Connor, when I grew up.

As you've seen, the mule deer is somewhat of an enigmatic animal. The last of the continent's three major deer species to arrive evolutionarily, it is the only one that is known to breed with the others and create hybrid deer. Mulies also prove themselves to be far less adaptable to catastrophic changes in their environment than either whitetails or blacktails, who both show the ability to thrive in our backyards.

Turn the page to learn more about the mule deer's history, its role in western expansion, and how, at the turn of the century, there were very few mulies left anywhere in the West. You'll see how population levels came to a crest in the mid-1960s and early 1970s—truly the "golden days" of mule deer hunting—only to drop again to a level in most states that gave game managers a horrible fright. Hopefully you'll gain an understanding of some of the major issues facing game managers as they try to work within the limitations of modern society to protect and enhance mule deer populations and habitat throughout the region, and how you might help.

The mule deer is one of North America's greatest, most noble big game animals. It is a joy to watch them in their natural environment, whether in the peaks of the Rocky Mountains or the Sierra Nevada range, the pinion/juniper high desert of southern Utah and northern Arizona, out on the Wyoming prairie, in the breaks along the Missouri river in Montana, or on the parched, cactus-filled deserts of old Mexico. It is a privilege to hunt them wherever they live.

I'm proud to say that I grew up to be a mule deer hunter. At the end of the 21st century, I hope that the proud and magnificent symbol of the West—the mature, big-bodied mule deer buck with oversized antlers—will still make young boys and girls dream.

LOOKING AHEAD

Once upon a time, mule deer herds dominated the Western big game scene. From the mid- to late-1950s through the late-1960s and early-1970s, mule deer hunting reached its peak. There were so many deer that tags were issued over-the-counter in virtually every state in the West. Some states even issued multiple tags. Hunting was, to be brief, incredible.

I can still remember pickup beds carrying several bucks back home, driven by neighbors and friends who traveled from southern California to Arizona, Utah and Colorado. Each hunting party brought home at least a couple of bucks that today would be considered deer of a lifetime. It was the heyday of the 30-incher, with bucks with incredible non-typical antlers relatively common.

In the mid-1970s, though, something happened. State wildlife biologists began to realize that their deer management programs—put in place to control once thriving deer herds—were not working. Instead, mule deer herds in many areas were in decline. So biologists, using the best tools available to them at the time, instituted programs they hoped would return mule deer herds to target levels and keep them there, improve buck/doe ratios, increase the average age of harvested bucks and increase fawn recruitment.

In most cases, their efforts didn't work. Across the board, deer numbers continued to drop, and herd compositions remained off target levels. In 1976, biologists from several western states met in Utah to discuss mule deer population declines. Several potential causes were identified, including drought, harsh winter weather,

predation, over-hunting, habitat loss and degradation, and competition from both livestock and other ungulates, including elk. It is interesting to note that at a similar meeting in Salt Lake City in early 1999, the list of problems remained essentially unchanged.

MULE DEER & WESTERN EXPANSION

There are few records of mule deer in the early days of western expansion. In *The Journals of Lewis and Clark*, Meriwether Lewis—who many believe named the mule deer—wrote that his men rarely saw mule deer, and then only in rough country. Other early settlers and explorers mirrored Lewis's views of mule deer. When Mormon settlers first arrived in the Salt Lake Valley in the mid-1800s, they found virtually no deer, and certainly not enough to feed them. (Note: some historians postulate that deer and other big-game herds were kept closely cropped by Native American hunters.) Throughout the West, from the gold fields of California to the Wyoming high country, from Montana's prairie lands to Arizona's high desert, mule deer were scarce.

As more and more settlers moved West, bringing with them voracious appetites and firearms, and as more and more Native Americans acquired firearms and shooting skills, all Western big game herds began to plummet. During the last half of the 19th century, increased hunting—remember, back then there was no such thing as a "hunting season" or "bag limit"—coupled with the brutal overgrazing of range lands by cattle and sheep, hammered mule deer herds. Something had to be done before deer were literally wiped out.

That something was a severe restriction on deer hunting. In 1899, New Mexico prohibited all deer hunting for five years. In 1908, Utah did the same thing. Other states soon followed suit. It is interesting to note that the first Utah deer season following the 1908 moratorium resulted in just 600 kills, and that in 1916, Utah had an estimated population of only 8,500 mule deer.

The states did what they could to help deer, which in those days was basically to restrict hunting. Cattle ranchers and sheep herders controlled the range, and they alone determined what was done with habitat—which was usually nothing as far as improvements go, except to construct some water holes and build fences. States soon undertook vigorous predator control campaigns, unmercifully targeting coyotes and mountain

There are few records of mule deer in the early days of western expansion by white settlers. During the last half of the 19th century, mule deer had been hunted down so badly that the first moratoriums on deer hunting were enacted.

lions. At first this produced positive results. However, on Arizona's Kaibab Plateau, the combination of predator annihilation and hunting restrictions led to a rapid overpopulation of deer, which soon literally ate themselves out of house and home. In a short time they destroyed their range, and a pair of harsh winters almost wiped out the entire herd.

STATE DEER MANAGEMENT MATURES

As the 20th century progressed, state game managers learned by the seat of their pants. Predator control was helpful, significantly reducing deer mortality. With the lesson of the Kaibab to guide them, game managers began to protect does and fawns, while allowing buck hunting. They soon learned that this was the way to control the rate of growth of deer herds. Also, livestock numbers were reduced on deer habitat, where they had all but eaten every browse plant down to bare earth. When this happened, new browse—the most succulent and nutritious for deer—overgrew grasses. Mule deer thrived.

By the Second World War, mule deer herds were booming across the West. But even then, a few astute game managers noticed that habitat degradation was beginning, telling them that they needed to cull deer herds back to avoid a population crash. It was time to institute the first doe seasons. However, sportsmen—

An increase in the number of predators in the West—including coyotes, but also mountain lions and wolves—has led to a sharp decline in mule deer numbers in some areas.

1968. In the 40 years between 1923 and 1963, Idaho's deer herd exploded from 23,000 to 315,000. Since the early '70s, though, no state has reported any type of surge in statewide muley numbers, though some local and regional herds expanded from time to time, due mainly to positive climatic conditions. But for the most part, mule deer herds in prime range—states like Wyoming, Utah and Idaho—continued to decline. In some places, this decline was drastic.

SPECIFIC MULE DEER CONCERNS

Some mule deer hunters blame the current status of mule deer herds on poor state management. To an extent, this is true. Hunters' groups have argued for years that states should cut back on deer hunting licenses. But because western state game departments get the bulk of their operating capital from the sale of nonresident hunting licenses, particularly deer and elk licenses, they have had strong reasons to sell more deer tags: They generate good revenue. But, unfortunately, selling unlimited deer tags is the best way there is to ensure that hunters hammer the deer.

Slowly but surely, game managers have realized that the days of selling unlimited buck mule deer tags are over. Utah first limited license sales in 1994, when it

who were told for decades that bucks-only hunting was the way to save deer—weren't buying it. They soundly rejected the idea. Deer herds continued to grow, but their habitat slowly but surely continued to erode.

This leads us back to the boom in deer hunting in the decade or so between the early-1960s and early-1970s. Many states noted peak muley populations between 1961 and 1963. Two states, Oregon and Washington, reported population highs in 1967 and

The last state to offer an unlimited number of over-the-counter mule deer licenses was Colorado, which ceased the practice in 1999. Game managers throughout the West realize that the mule deer resource is a fragile one, in need of careful nurturing in the 21st century.

Mule Deer—Western Challenge

limited licenses to 97,000, down from 220,000, and strictly controlled the number of bucks that could be killed. Colorado was the last state to eliminate unlimited tags, with 1999 the first year that all deer tags were issued by drawing, with the number of total tags that could be issued capped. Colorado estimates that, in so doing, it will lose some $5 million in revenue. But it's the right decision. When implemented, there were an estimated 500,000 mule deer, 20 percent fewer than a decade before. In certain parts of the state, only 35 to 40 fawns can be found for every 100 does, well below the levels needed to maintain population levels.

Mule deer herds are increasingly being squeezed out by urban sprawl in areas of the West where human populations are exploding. As more people move into deer country, critical habitat is disappearing, leading to a drop in overall deer numbers.

The problem is complex, the answers equally so. There's no doubt that competition from other animals, especially the West's booming elk herds, has displaced mule deer in many areas. Predation, especially in states that have outlawed poisoning and trapping of coyotes and given the mountain lion complete protection, is a growing concern. The introduction of wolves—another aggressive predator with complete protection—to many parts of the West will not help. There are other troubles.

However, all those explanations are overshadowed by what is widely considered the number-one reason for the declining mule deer numbers—changes in habitat, both natural and man-made.

"The real and most serious cause of mule deer herd declines is primarily the disappearance of what we call good deer habitat, or the primary browse species that deer are dependent on," says biologist Wayne Long, president of Multiple Use Managers, a private group that contracts with private landowners to help them improve game habitat on their lands. Long is also a member of the Mule Deer Foundation board. Long said there are numerous reasons for this, but the most important are the following:

- Wildfires are no longer allowed to burn unchecked. "Instead of browse plants being set back and started anew, they are allowed to grow and age to where they are either not available and/or not palatable to the deer, or eventually the browse is crowded out by a forest canopy," Long says.

- Changes in range management policies on both public and private range lands. "What has happened is that range lands are being managed for grass and grazing animals—including elk—better than they have been for a long time," Long explains. "Good grass cover can actually crowd out browse species like mule deer, as well as prevent seedling establishment. The snowball here is that, as elk increase, mule deer decrease."

- Mule deer winter ranges have declined due to reservoir construction, the encroachment of home sites and development of highways. "Unfortunately, it has been found that mule deer are a site-specific animal to their home ranges, and adapt very poorly to unfamiliar areas," Long says. "When they lose their home range, it is tough for them to move to a new range and thrive."

Examples of human encroachment abound in the West. The Front Range of Colorado, once one of the mule deer's strongholds, is fast becoming one giant suburb. On Utah's Wasatch Front, housing developments continue to crawl up into foothill canyons and draws where mule deer once wintered. In Washington and Oregon, orchard growers have fenced the fringes

Mule deer are primarily browsers and need rough forage to thrive. Many areas of the West today are being managed for grass, which is great for elk but not for mulies.

of large rivers so blacktails and mule deer cannot nibble on their trees. These orchards cover what was once invaluable deer winter range.

In many areas of the West, it is possible to find habitat that looks like a perfect place for mule deer to thrive that is empty. The reason is simple—it is only seasonal range, with the winter range necessary to support mule deer herds now nothing more than a housing development, industrial complex or recreational development, like a golf course or ski resort.

- Prolonged periods of drought, like the one that existed for seven years prior to 1993, is tougher on browse plants than it is on grasses. Drought years make it tough for mule deer to find the high-quality browse they need to stay strong, and for young deer to survive. And tough winters also take a serious toll on deer numbers.

"When bad winters came or summer droughts made it difficult for deer to survive, you notice a 'stair step effect,'" Long says. "After the deer recover from weather-related mortality, their numbers peak at a lower number than previously, and the declines the next time are steeper than before," Long says. "Basically, mule deer habitat is stressed, and the deer are stressed, especially in winter."

THE FUTURE

The question is, what can be done to protect mule deer herds from further degradation, and/or to increase their numbers across the board?

The answers are complex, given the expansion of people into the West's traditional mule deer habitat. The bottom line is that some of the negative trends on the range might be reversed, but the general population may not be willing to pay the price, both socially and financially. Wayne Long has some ideas:

"While deer habitat lost to reservoir building, home construction and highways will never be reversed, we have to find a way to reduce mule deer habitat losses when new construction occurs," he says.

"I also firmly believe that fire suppression programs need to be rethought," Long points out. "The idea that every fire in the wild needs to be suppressed as soon as possible doesn't help mule deer. While fire can be an important management tool, it needs to be used during controlled burning on both public and private lands. Finding the dollars to do this on public lands, and convincing the public that controlled burns that both enhance habitat and reduce the risk of catastrophic fires later on, are both tough political issues."

Long also believes that public grazing policies that favor grasslands over browse plants—and thus, favor cattle and elk over deer—must be changed. "Deer need browse, and in areas where there is little browse or high numbers of elk, mule deer will be out competed on the winter range," Long says. "It's that simple."

Some biologists don't consider predator control to be a viable deer management tool. Long disagrees. "I think that today, with our reduced mule deer populations and on specific properties, it may be wise to keep mule deer predators, such as coyotes and mountain

The loss of critical winter range habitat, as well as the blocking of traditional migration corridors from summer to winter range by highways and housing developments, is a real threat to mule populations across the West.

lions, at low population levels. This includes both public and private lands," Long says. In the situation mule deer are in, every fawn counts. If taking a predator off the range might save a fawn, the trade is a good one. Predators are survivors too; a little pressure on their ranks won't destroy them.

"For these reasons, we have to recognize that, at least on public lands, we will probably never have the mule deer herds we once had," Long explains. "To increase deer numbers will require specific and well-planned management over a number of years. Unfortunately, due to economic and political reasons, more and more of the necessary habitat work, and hence, the increase of deer herds, will be on private, not public, lands."

THE FUTURE OF MULE DEER HUNTING

All this doesn't mean that mule deer herds—and mule deer hunting—are in the tank. Not by any means.

Mule deer hunters will continue to find good hunting throughout the deer's range, at least in the near term. What all this does mean is that the game is changing, and changing rapidly. The chances of a repeat of the "good old days" of the 1960s on public lands across the West is virtually nil. In the 21st century, the successful mule deer hunter will need to stay abreast of changing developments across the deer's range, educate himself as much as he can about the deer's likes and dislikes, learn new hunting techniques (including, perhaps, how to shoot a bow or muzzleloader) and learn the ins and outs of the each state's special-draw systems. He may also find it worthwhile to consider hunting private land either by hiring a guide or paying a trespass fee.

One thing is certain. Mule deer are a fragile resource, in need of all the care and nurturing sportsmen can give them. It will take people like us—those who love mule deer, as well as love to hunt them—who are willing to give our time and money, and use our political influence to help shape public-land-use policy, to ensure that the great symbol of the West, the large-antlered, mature mule deer buck, is here for our children's children to enjoy.

The Mule Deer Foundation

*I*f you're a mule deer and/or blacktail hunter, you should belong to the Mule Deer Foundation (MDF). This organization is dedicated to the conservation and enhancement of mule deer and blacktail populations and the deer's habitat throughout North America. Local chapters hold annual fundraising banquets, which are always fun, and the money raised goes to directly to on-the-ground projects that benefit mule deer and deer habitat throughout the West. Chapter members also volunteer their time and sweat to perform much of this habitat work. The Mule Deer Foundation works closely with state game departments in all phases of mule deer work, including habitat enhancement and conducting herd counts.

The membership is a diverse one, including hunters, outfitters, game department personnel and businesses big and small. Annual individual memberships cost about $25, and include a subscription to MDF's classy quarterly magazine, *Mule Deer*.

For more information, contact the Mule Deer Foundation, 1005 Terminal Way, Suite 170, Reno, NV 89502; (775)322-6558 or (888)375-DEER.

THE
MULE DEER
FOUNDATION

APPENDIX & INDEX

APPENDIX

If there is one theme that came across strongly in this book, I hope it is this: that the consistently successful mule deer hunter is the informed hunter. Information doesn't grow on trees, however. It is gathered by research. Here is where you can get started.

STATE GAME DEPARTMENTS

In addition to writing or calling individual game departments, you can also glean information from various state's World Wide Web sites. They can be found at http://www.state.az.us (the "az" is for Arizona; substitute the two-letter abbreviation of the state you're interested in here.)

ALASKA DEPARTMENT OF FISH AND GAME
P.O. Box 25526
Juneau, AK 99802
(907) 465-4112

ARIZONA GAME AND FISH DEPARTMENT
2222 W. Greenway Rd.
Phoenix, AZ 85023
(602) 942-3000

CALIFORNIA DEPARTMENT OF FISH AND GAME
1416 - 9th St.
Sacramento, CA 94244
(916) 227-2244

COLORADO DIVISION OF WILDLIFE
6060 Broadway
Denver, CO 80216
(303) 291-7299

IDAHO DEPARTMENT OF FISH AND GAME
P.O. Box 25
Boise, ID 83707
(208) 334-3700

KANSAS DEPARTMENT OF WILDLIFE AND PARKS
900 SW Jackson St., Ste. 202
Topeka, KS 66612
(913) 296-2281

MONTANA DEPARTMENT OF FISH, WILDLIFE AND PARKS
1420 E. 6th
Helena, MT 59620
(406) 444-2535

NEBRASKA GAME AND PARKS COMMISSION
2200 N. 33rd St.
Lincoln, NE 68503
(402) 471-0641

NEVADA DEPARTMENT OF WILDLIFE
P.O. Box 10678
Reno, NV 89520
(702) 688-1500

NEW MEXICO GAME AND FISH DEPARTMENT
State Capitol, Villagra Bldg.
Santa Fe, NM 87503
(505) 827-7911

North Dakota Game and Fish Department

100 N. Bismarck Expressway
Bismarck, ND 58501
(701) 328-6300

Oklahoma Department of Wildlife Conservation

1801 N. Lincoln
Oklahoma City, OK 73105
(405) 521-2739

Oregon Department of Fish and Wildlife

P.O. Box 59
Portland, OR 97207
(503) 872-5268

South Dakota Department of Game, Fish and Parks

523 E. Capitol
Pierre, SD 57501
(605) 773-3381

Texas Parks and Wildlife Department

4200 Smith School Rd.
Austin, TX 78744
(512) 389-4800

Utah Wildlife Division

1596 W. North Temple
Salt Lake City, UT 84116
(801) 538-4700

Washington Department of Wildlife

600 Capitol Way N.
Olympia, WA 98501
(360) 902-2200

Wyoming Game and Fish Department

5400 Bishop Blvd.
Cheyenne, WY 82206
(307) 777-4600

Topographic Maps

You can often obtain topographic maps from backpacking stores and some larger hunting shops throughout the West. You can also order maps from the U.S. Geological Survey, Distribution Branch, Federal Center, Denver, CO 80225; phone (303) 236-5900. First call and ask for a state order map, off of which specific individual maps can be ordered.

DeLorme Mapping Company publishes the popular state-by-state atlas and gazetteer map books. These books have more than a hundred pages of quadrangle maps that cover an entire state. They're great for beginning the planning and research phase of a hunt, as well as for navigating around the state once you get there. Their scale (1:150,000, or about $2^1/2$ miles per inch) isn't fine enough to permit using them to pinpoint potential hot spots or identify specific private property boundaries, but they are a constant companion in my office library and in my truck.

You can find the atlas and gazetteer map books for your own state in most bookstores and sporting goods stores. Information on ordering volumes not available locally can be obtained from DeLorme Mapping Company, Two DeLorme Drive, P.O. Box 298, Yarmouth, ME 04096; (800) 452-5931, or (207) 865-4171.

National Forests

These regional headquarters of the U.S. Forest Service can provide a complete list of national forests within their region. From these regional forest headquarters offices you can obtain current information on logging operations, fires, etc., as well as purchase specific national forest maps. The U.S. Forest Service, and its regional offices nationwide, can also be found on the World Wide Web at www.fs.fed.us.

Region 1 (Montana, northern Idaho):
(406) 329-3089; (406) 329-2411 fax

Region 2 (Colorado, part of Wyoming):
(303) 275-5350; (303) 275-5366 fax

Region 3 (Arizona, New Mexico):
(505) 842-3076; (505) 476-3300 fax

Region 4 (Nevada, southern Idaho, Western Wyoming): (801) 625-5262; (801) 625-5240 fax

Region 5 (California):
(415) 705/1837; (415) 705-1097 fax

Region 6 (Oregon, Washington):
(503) 808-2971; (503) 326-5044 fax

BUREAU OF LAND MANAGEMENT (BLM)

Information on current land status, logging operations, fires, etc., as well as maps of BLM lands are available from these regional offices. Each state's BLM World Wide Web site is found at www.ak.blm.gov ("ak" is for Alaska; substitute the two-letter abbreviation of the state you're interested in here.)

Alaska:	(907) 271-5960
Arizona:	(602) 417-9200
California:	(916) 978-4400
Colorado:	(303) 239-3600
Idaho:	(208) 373-3930
Montana:	(406) 255-2782
Nevada:	(702) 861-6400
New Mexico:	(505) 438-7400
Oregon and Washington:	(503) 952-6027
Utah:	(801) 539-4001
Washington:	(see Oregon)
Wyoming:	(307) 775-6256

STATE OUTFITTER ASSOCIATIONS

There are a truckload of excellent mule deer guides and outfitters who will give you a great hunt for your hard-earned money. There are also a few fly-by-nights who will rip you off. Before any money changes hands, be sure any guide or outfitter you're considering is licensed and bonded by the state in which he wants to take you hunting.

How to check up on this? Contact each state and ask. Here's who to contact:

In Alaska (Division of Occupational Licensing), Arizona (Game and Fish Department), California (License and Revenue Branch), Kansas (Department of Wildlife and Parks), Nevada (Division of Wildlife, Law Enforcement Branch), New Mexico (Game and Fish Department) and North Dakota (Licensing Bureau, Game and Fish Department), contact each agency at the address and telephone number listed earlier under "State Game Departments."

Other state regulatory agencies are:

COLORADO DEPARTMENT OF REGULATORY AGENTS,
1560 Broadway, #1340
Denver, CO 80202
(303) 894-7778

IDAHO OUTFITTERS AND GUIDES LICENSING BOARD
1365 N. Orchard Room 172
Boise, ID 83706
(208) 327-7380

MONTANA BOARD OF OUTFITTERS
Arcade Bldg.
Lower Level, 111 N. Jackson
Helena, MT 59620
(406) 444-3738

OREGON STATE MARINE BOARD
P.O. Box 14145
Salem, OR 97309
(503) 378-8587

SOUTH DAKOTA PROFESSIONAL GUIDES AND OUTFITTERS ASSOCIATION
P.O. Box 703
Pierre, SD 57501
(605) 945-2928

WASHINGTON OUTFITTERS AND GUIDES ASSOCIATION
22845 NE 8th - Ste. 331
Redmond, WA 98053
(877) 275-4964

Wyoming State Board of Outfitters and Professional Guides

1750 Westland Road, Ste. 166
Cheyenne, WY 82002
(307) 777-5323

Nebraska, Oklahoma, Texas and Utah do not have these types of organizations.

Booking Agents

Booking agents are really hunt brokers. They work on commission from the outfitters they represent. Using one does not cost you, the client, any more money than if you'd booked a hunt directly with the outfitter himself. Booking agents can also help mediate any problems that arise between clients and outfitters, sometimes offering discounts on future hunts if your dream hunt turns sour for reasons beyond your control. They want you to be happy so you'll book with them again. However, beware of fly-by-night booking agents. There are a million and one part-time booking agents out there, many of whom are in the business more for the fringe benefits than the success and satisfaction of the hunting public. One good source of quality booking agents is the American Association of Professional Hunting and Fishing Consultants (AAPH-FC), whose member agents meet professional conduct criteria. More information and a member's list can be obtained by calling (717) 652-4374.

Information, Licensing Services

There are two excellent sources of information on all western hunting, and especially mule deer hunting, you can use for a small fee. I've used both, and have been very satisfied. They are:

Garth Carter's Hunter Services, P.O. Box 45, Minersville, UT 84752; (435) 386-1020; (435) 386-1090 fax; on the World Wide Web at www.huntinfool.com. Carter is a former Utah state game biologist and serious big-game hunter. His service publishes a monthly newsletter filled with information on the very best western hunts for all species, including mulies, state-by-state updates, trophy units updates, limited-entry hunts drawing odds, harvest statistics and more.

Carter also helps members with their nonresident applications, includes information on private land hunting and ranch leases and works with a handful of topnotch outfitters as a booking agent. At $100 per year, it's a great bargain.

United States Outfitters Professional Licensing Service, P.O. Box 4204, Taos, NM 87571; (800) 845-9929. George Taulman started the first western licensing service. For a nominal fee his staff will do the research for you, complete your applications for the best western hunts for whatever species you're interested in, including mule deer. If you don't draw the hunt you're dreaming of one year and choose to do so, Taulman will continue to apply for you to hunt the same hunt year after year, helping you accumulate the bonus points you need to finally pick the tag. Taulman also offers top-quality guided hunting in several states; however, if you draw a tag by using his licensing service, you are not obligated to hunt with his guides, but are free to hunt on your own if you wish.

INDEX